Who Am I?

Irma Zaleski

Who Am I?

NOVALIS

Cover design and layout: Renée Longtin
Cover image: icon of the Baptism of the Lord by Marysia Kowalczyk of
Madonna House

Business Office:
Novalis
49 Front Street East, 2nd Floor
Toronto, Ontario, Canada
M5E 1B3

Phone: 1-800-387-7164
Fax: (514) 278-3030
E-mail: cservice@novalis-inc.com
www.novalis.ca

Library and Archives Canada Cataloguing in Publication
Zaleski, Irma
    Who am I? / Irma Zaleski.
ISBN 2-89507-568-9
    1. Self–Religious aspects–Christianity. I. Title.
BT713.Z34 2005   233   C2005-900383-9

Printed in Canada.

We acknowledge the financial support of the Government of Canada
through the Book Publishing Industry Development Program (BPIDP)
for our publishing activities.

5 4 3 2 1   09 08 07 06 05

Contents

Preface

As I wrote my last book, *Who Is God?* – a reflection on the mystery of God – I knew I would have to write another one on the mystery of "I." For as all religious traditions and most philosophers agree, we cannot consider the meaning of the mystery of God without, at the same time, considering the meaning and purpose of our own existence. These two questions are inseparable: they are two parts of the same ontological mystery that lies at the core of all being.

Thus, *Who Is God?* and *Who Am I?* are really two parts of one book, two sides of the same coin. As we begin to experience more deeply the mystery of God's presence in the world and at the core of ourselves, in our own hearts, we also begin to know ourselves more fully. We cannot do one without the other.

Our human reality seems to be stretched out between the earthly reality of everyday life and the divine reality that lies beyond: always there, always calling to us and yet always, it seems, beyond our reach. There is a gap between our finiteness and the infinity of God that we cannot cross. The two sides of the mystery, it appears to us, can never touch.

Yet one day we may realize – not only as an idea but as the reality of our own inner life – that the gap has been bridged. Christ has entered it and joined the two sides of the mystery together once and for all. We can be at home in each.

Christians have reflected on this amazing truth for centuries and have tried to express it in teaching, in prayer, in the lives of the saints, in music and art. The icon – the sacred art of the Orthodox Church – has no other purpose than to make this truth of heaven and earth joined together in the person of Christ visible and present to us.

No icon expresses this truth more clearly and specifically than the icon of the Baptism of Christ that appears on the cover of this book. Christ descends into the River Jordan – flowing deep and dark between the two shores of reality – making them one. There will be time to reflect on this icon more fully in a later chapter, but it seemed worthwhile to mention it here, for the truth that it expresses is central to this book. As Christians, we can approach the mystery of ourselves only in the presence of God who, in Christ, has entered the depths of our own reality and abides at the heart of our being.

Who Am I?

As a young teenager, I once asked an older friend whom I greatly admired, "What does 'self' mean?" She explained, "When you say 'I see,' or 'I know,' or 'I am,' this I is your self." "Yes, but what is it?" I persisted. "How can I tell you that?" she asked. "I am not you!"

I remember feeling puzzled and strangely stirred by that conversation. For the first time, I became consciously aware of the mystery of my own "I-ness," the uniqueness and singularity of my self. I realized that nobody else was this "I" that I was, and that I could never be the "I" they were. All others, no matter how beloved, remained outside, at the door, unable to come in. They could shut themselves against me just as I could, and often did, shut myself against them. This was a frightening mystery to me.

Nearly sixty years later, it still is. I still experience great amazement, even awe, when I realize how deep and unbridgeable is the abyss of not-knowing that separates us from each other. There have been moments of insight, of communion with the people I loved, but such moments pass quickly and I still do not know how to explain myself, even to them. I can tell them about myself — my story, my thoughts and emotions, my wants and needs – but I cannot explain to them the "I," the core, the heart of my being. I cannot even explain it to myself.

This dilemma, I believe, is one we all face. Sooner or later we all realize that there is more to us than what we are now, and what we have been. We suspect – perhaps even hope – that we do not know something essential about ourselves, and we need to search for this missing piece. As Carl Jung said, we are all in search of ourselves.

The task of all religions and all genuine spiritual traditions is to lead us on this search of self-discovery. Although their understanding of "self" may differ radically from each other, all agree that our goal in life is to find it, to free it from the distortions and self-deceptions that obscure it, to come to terms with it and to let it grow into who we were created to become.

The true goal of our search is not to make us wiser or more interesting or even more "holy," but to make us real. As the great St. Anthony is reported to have said to one of his disciples, "When you die and appear before the judgment seat of God, you will not be asked if you have become another Anthony, but whether you have become truly yourself."

The search for the truth of ourselves has been compared to entering a desert – probably not the physical desert, a place of sand and dry rocks (although a few of us may be called to do that, too) but the inner desert: the desert at the heart of our being. For me, this has meant entering and exploring my own aloneness, my separateness from others, an emptiness that nothing in life seemed to fill. I had to discover that this desert was not a place of final rejection and defeat but a place where I could encounter God.

It is this search that I have chosen to write about here – not only because it has been the main preoccupation of my own life, but also because it has taught me something that I hope can be helpful to others. Even though we all have to struggle to find the truth of ourselves on our unique path, the goal of each is common to us all and thus our struggle is much more than our own. In an amazing and mysterious way, our own unique truth points beyond ourselves to the one Divine Reality from whom all human uniqueness – our personhood – flows, and whom, however "darkly," it reflects.

Through a Child's Eyes

A few months ago I was sitting on a couch with my eight-year-old grandson, Joseph, who was showing me some of his drawings. Among them I noticed a small picture of a woman's face. "This looks very much like your mommy," I said. "It is my mommy!" he replied. I looked at the drawing a little longer. "But it also reminds me a bit of myself," I added.

Joseph looked very closely at me for a minute or so. "Yes, you do look like Mommy," he concluded. "Except you have bags under your eyes, but that is because you are old." Then he lightly pulled the skin on my face. "And your skin is kind of wrinkly. That is also because you are old!"

I was deeply touched by my grandson's comments. How I would love to be able to look at myself that way! I thought. Most of us would want to see ourselves like that: without like or dislike, without judgment – simply to look at what was there. We all probably were able to do this as children, but now that we are grown up, we seem to have forgotten how.

Since I became a grandmother, I have often thought about this forgetting. I am always filled with joy and wonder at the uniqueness of each of my grandchildren. They are still so little and yet are already so different from each other. Each possesses his or her own character, likes and dislikes, talents and gifts. They are so aware, so open to the world around them, and yet so simple and clear in their perception of it; they are so trustful and unafraid of seeing with their own eyes, having their own thoughts, being their own person or self.

Young children have not yet formed any self-concept – any idea of who they "should" or should not be. They seem open to every possibility that presents itself; they are capable of growing into their own true self just by being themselves, without having to be forced or trained to it by others. It is this aspect of childhood, I think, that Christ alluded to when he said, "Unless you become like children, you cannot enter the Kingdom of Heaven" (Matthew 18:3).

I realize, as never before, that it is this simple, truthful self – their true personhood created in the image of God – that will be their life's work, their true vocation, to nourish, to enjoy and, at the end, to surrender into the hands of God. They will have to defend it when it is threatened, remember it when it is forgotten or obscured, and find it again when it has been denied or lost for a while, as it surely will be.

It seems to be an unavoidable result of our human condition that, sooner or later, we all lose the directness and innocence we possessed as children and become strangers to ourselves. As we grow older and more aware of our total dependence on the outside world, we learn to judge, doubt and distrust ourselves. We may be haunted by the fear of being not good enough, not strong or clever enough; we may feel we have failed to meet others' expectations.

In order to earn others' respect and admiration, we may think we need to take on roles that do not fit our inner aspirations or hopes. We may begin to look at the world, and ourselves, through other people's eyes, to think other people's thoughts and speak other people's words. In the end, we forget how to be truly ourselves.

Acquiring an Ego

This process of self-forgetting may be interpreted as acquiring what modern psychology calls an ego. From that perspective, the ego is understood to be an inner mechanism the mind develops, most often unconsciously, to bring all the irrational aspects of our being under control and to allow us to adapt to the demands of growing up and taking our place in the adult world.

Self-forgetting may also be viewed as a process of developing a personality or persona (a Greek word for the mask that actors wore to indicate the role they were playing). We, too, often feel a need to put on a mask in order to play a role we must or want to assume in society. Thus, both "persona" and "ego" may be understood to refer to our social identity: the way our self, our "I," expresses itself, relates to others and is viewed by them, or presents itself to the world.

To acquire an ego or a persona does not therefore necessarily mean forgetting or denying our own truth. Rather, it may involve an indispensable and thus "natural" process of training our social self.[1] In this process, our parents and our community prepare us for the reality of our existence in the world, an essential step on the way to adulthood.

For we do need to learn and develop our social skills, just as we need to develop all other aspects of our minds, bodies and souls. We need to learn to control our emotions and to put aside our own personal needs and desires for the sake of a higher good. We need to learn how to play our proper role in our families and in our communities, even when we may prefer to do something else. Sometimes we are called upon to display wisdom, courage or strength that we do not possess – not only to fulfill our role but also to protect ourselves or others from harm. Sometimes we have to learn how to pretend, perhaps even lie.

This real and often agonizing need to hide the truth is something that even young children may have to learn. As a child in Nazi-occupied Poland during World War II, I remember confessing to a priest that I had to tell lies nearly every day; even my mother told me so. I had to lie about her resistance activities, about buying things on the black market, about attending a forbidden Polish school, and many other things.

The priest listened very seriously but then reassured me that my mother was right and that these kinds of "lies" were not lies at all. We do not have to tell the whole truth, he told me, to those who have no right to know it. And the Nazis certainly had no such right. In fact, he added, to tell them about such things would be not only unnecessary but also wrong, as it could seriously hurt others.

I was comforted by this advice, although not sure whether it was true. It seemed to contradict everything I had been taught about lying: that it was bad and shameful and that there was no excuse for it. Looking back, however, I cannot see what else my mother or the priest could have told me. It might have been better, and much more spiritually true, if they had simply said, "Lying is not good – it is bad for you – but there are times when we must do what we must do. God will understand." But I'm not sure a child would have understood or been satisfied with such an answer.

Years later, Mother Thekla,[2] an Orthodox nun, cast some light on this situation: "You do not always have to, nor should you, inform others of what you really think or feel or believe," she told me. "You do not always need to explain yourself to others. You may even feel forced to tell lies. That is the tragedy of living in this world. But it is essential never to forget what the truth is and to hold on to it in your own mind."

Just Pretending

Such a distinction between lying and withholding the truth is very difficult for children – and most adults – to make. It requires a level of self-understanding that we as adults possess only rarely. We do not like to admit, even to ourselves, that we are pretending or telling lies. We may prefer to deny and resent it when we are told that we are not being true to ourselves or that we are playing games.

Children, on the other hand, unless life has taught them otherwise, seem to know instinctively how to play all kinds of games; it is an important part of their lives. By taking on different roles and putting them aside again, they learn – not consciously, of course, but at a much deeper level, that these are only roles and can be and need to be put aside after a while. They become introduced to an essential aspect of being a human person: the need to learn to distinguish between what is real and must be held onto, and what is assumed and may be let go of. They imagine many different identities for themselves, take on a range of roles and act them out with total absorption and interest, but they do not forget who they truly are. They know they are "just pretending," as my grandchildren say.

My grandson Sam often played one especially interesting game when he was little. He would announce that now he would not be Sam but some other boy (not an imaginary boy but a cousin or a friend). Then he would hand out appropriate roles to the rest of us. His parents were to be the other boy's parents, his baby brother played the other child's brother (or sister, for that seemed immaterial) and I would become the other's grandma. Even the family dog would be assigned a new role.

These games went on till Sam decided to be Sam again. It had to be his decision to begin and his decision to end it. I was always struck by the importance he seemed to attach to this aspect of the game. He was, it seemed to me, exploring being "not Sam" – being another – but he always remained in control of it and never seemed to lose sight of his real identity.

This, I think, is true of most children's games. Through games, children learn and practise the essential social skill of assuming different roles in different circumstances without becoming stuck in the game. They explore and try on the adult world without forgetting who they truly are.

For some children, however, playing games may become a much more confusing and potentially dangerous activity. Children who have been unloved or abused, who have been taught to believe that they are not good enough as they are – that they are "bad" – may play their games not as a way of having fun and exploring the world, but as a way of escaping the reality of their helplessness and fear. They may get lost in their games, fantasies or dreams; they may begin to confuse them with reality and lose the sense of their own true identity. It may become extremely difficult in later life for such children to find their own truth again.

But even for children who have had a basically happy and healthy childhood, game playing may become much less enjoyable and, at times, even threatening. If their parents try too hard to direct and dictate the kind of roles the children should explore in their play, especially when these roles do not fit their own true interests and needs, children may begin to resent and rebel against their parents – especially when the children realize that they are expected not only to play these roles now, for fun, but for the rest of their lives.

Throwing Irons over Fences

O ne day, when I was four or five years old, my father gave me a small toy iron, a replica of the one my mother had. I can still remember it clearly: a lovely little brass thing, glittering in the sunlight. But instead of thanking him, I ran out into the garden and threw his gift over the fence into our neighbour's garden. My father, looking angry, searched for it among the bushes behind the fence but, strangely enough, he never found it.

What possessed me to do such a rude and un-grateful thing? Looking back, I think it must have been an early sign of my rebellion against the "little woman" role that I did not want and that I felt was being forced upon me. I was often told that unless I learned to behave "like a lady," I would be a disgrace and an old maid for sure, for who would ever marry such a hooligan? Such comments always made me very angry, although at the time I could not have said why.

Not all children, of course, resist and rebel against the roles that they are expected to assume. Many find such roles natural and easy to embrace. My own daughter, although I never told her to behave "like a lady" or encouraged her to take an interest in "womanly" activities, grew up to be very good at both, and to have a career as well. In fact, she has told me more than once that she would have appreciated my encouraging her a little more in those activities when she was a child. Too often she had to go to her best friend's mother for advice about doing her hair up or baking a cake.

But I also know that there are many people like me who, as children, could not fit comfortably into the patterns expected of them. Some felt diminished and thwarted by adults' disregard for their own identity. They may have kicked up a fuss now and then and thrown a few unwanted irons over a few fences; they may have remained rebellious and angry for the rest of their lives, although it would be very difficult for them to say why. If they have not yet understood the nature of their own inner struggle, they may continue the process and impose unsuitable roles on their own children.

Realizing we have perpetuated an injustice may be the heaviest cross of parenthood. And yet, we must not become too worried or inhibited as parents. There is no way that we could or should bring up our children without training them in the way that we believe will help them to find their right role in life. We have to do our best and trust our children to find their own true way, as I once heard the Tibetan Buddhist teacher Chogyam Trungpa tell one young parent.

This man had asked Trungpa how to avoid burdening his small son with an ego without making him into "a little savage." "It is your job as a parent to give your child an ego," Trungpa replied, "for he would not be able to survive one day in this world without it. He will just have to find his own way of going beyond it, as you are doing. And that will be good for him!"

Egotism

Once we are grown up, no matter how much we may rebel and protest, the pressures of everyday life – the need to belong, to be accepted and approved, or just to make a living – make it difficult to hold onto the simplicity of self-awareness and self-acceptance we had as children. We may have identified so completely with the ego we have assumed, that it may seem inconceivable that we could ever be any other "self."

From that perspective, serving and protecting the needs of our ego may become the highest goal, the only real goal, of all our activities and relationships. We may come to believe that any injury to our ego leaves us with no life at all. And so, we grasp at whatever gives us pleasure, whatever makes us feel good – physically, psychologically and emotionally – and reject whatever causes us pain.

This is the great perversion of egotism: we become convinced that the well-being and survival of our own ego – our outer man, as St. Paul seems to have called it (2 Corinthians 4:16) – is the highest goal of existence, and that its desires and needs are the most important in the universe. When this happens our inner self becomes spiritually blind, unable to see its own true reality.

It is only then that we may rightly say that we have forgotten our true self and acquired a false self: we have identified ourselves with one aspect of our human reality and mistaken it for the whole. Our outer self has become the flesh, lost and entangled in the world of illusion and sin, to use the terms of the early Church.

From that perspective, egotism is understood as the sin of selfishness or self-love: the root from which all sins spring. It is the fundamental perversion of our true reality, turning our whole being upside-down. Blinded by egotism, we put our distorted, selfish ego first; what should be first – the true self that God gave us at creation – we put last. The Christian path of holiness is a path of restoring the right order in which we view our own being and live our lives: we put what is important – what is truly real in ourselves – at the centre of our lives.

The sin of selfishness should never be confused with the true love of self that we are all called to learn. True love of self is, in fact, our duty as Christians and an indispensable part of the commandment of love. We cannot love others as we love ourselves if we do not love ourselves first; if we do not protect our own inner truth; if we have forgotten or denied our true self. It is not our true self that we must hate but our egotism: the perversion and blindness of self-love.

The Dangers of Egotism

Egotism is a dangerous state of being: dangerous to others, to ourselves and to our whole spiritual life. As Choygam Trungpa has said, an unenlightened person – a person blind to his or her true reality – is more dangerous than an atom bomb. Those who have become convinced that their ego is the only self they have – their only reality – will defend this ego with every means at their disposal, regardless of the consequences.

It is the unenlightened ones who become tyrants, abusive parents and every other kind of bully who seeks to dominate and humiliate others. They can abuse and pervert every aspect of their lives and use it to serve their egotism. They turn love into possessiveness and dominance, family loyalty into arrogance and pride, patriotism into chauvinism, religion into intolerance.

It is also they who often succumb – as have so many over the ages in all cultures and religious traditions – to the most threatening and extreme manifestation of the spiritual danger of egotism: the terrible plague of fanaticism. At the root of fanaticism lies the conviction that possession of religious truth gives those who are blessed with it not only the right but the obligation to impose it on others. Fanatics are convinced that they have been given a special licence to hate: not only to despise but to persecute, and even to kill, those who do not accept their "truth." And all in the name of God.

Egotism, however, is not always directed at others; it may also be directed at ourselves. It may express itself as a painful and debilitating sense of dissatisfaction with ourselves, or as a sense of guilt. Deep in our minds, we may still nurse the childish feeling that we have failed: that we have never quite achieved the standards set for us by others, never quite fulfilled the role we were expected to play. In other words, we may believe that our ego, which we have now learned to identify as our original true self, has failed to meet the required standards.

This state of mind becomes even more dangerous and fraught with emotional and psychological suffering for those whose early training in their adult roles was imposed without love or understanding, perhaps even with cruelty and abuse. Such children often turn against themselves the evil done to them, and may carry a burden of shame and guilt for the rest of their lives. They may feel responsible for their imperfections and failures, or place impossible demands on themselves to appease those who have rejected them.

Many of us, including those who were happy and loved as children, may have such a rejected child hiding in us and may experience a similar hunger for love and acceptance from others. Even the most loving and well-intentioned parents are not always able to resist placing too many expectations on their children and setting unattainable goals for them. Few of us, it seems, whatever disguises we might adopt, are really happy with ourselves or convinced that we are all that we should be, that we are acceptable just as we are and do not have to deserve to be loved.

Dependency

S uch self-doubt may cause us to fall into another danger of egotism: dependency. We may develop a compulsive need to prove to ourselves and others that we are worthy of love, spending the rest of our lives searching for a person, a place, a community or movement where we will at last feel that we belong.

From that perspective, dependency may seriously endanger and distort not only our psychological and emotional life, but our spiritual life as well. We may attach ourselves to spiritual leaders or groups not to learn from them or to become involved in a common spiritual effort, but to seek acceptance and love. Genuine spiritual teachers are well aware of the danger of such dependency, both to their disciples and to themselves, and tend to discourage it.

Catherine Doherty, the foundress of Madonna House – a lay Catholic community located in Combermere, Ontario, a few miles from where I now live – told me once that whenever she saw people beginning to cling to her, she felt compelled to discourage them, sometimes quite roughly, because she realized the danger dependency was to them and to her. She knew it would be very easy for her to begin to use such dependency in ways that would feed her own need for others' admiration and subservience. This, I remember thinking, was her way of saying that she, too, could have become as dangerous as an atom bomb.

It may be hard to see dependency as an expression of egotism. It may appear, rather, to be a sign of humility: of humble acknowledgment of our own weakness and our need for love. But true humility does not lie merely in realizing and not hiding our weaknesses and faults, and even less in using them to manipulate others to gain their acceptance and love. It does not lie in trying to get their attention by being "bad."

When I was a young girl, in Grade 3 or 4, the nun who taught us catechism had us cut out big cardboard hearts on which we were to stick a red sticker for each good act we performed and a black one for any bad or selfish act. We had to bring our cardboard heart to school at the end of each week to show how well or badly we had done.

This, I remember, became a game, even an obsession with us. We competed madly to get the greatest number of red stickers each week. Needless to say, there were very few black ones marring our cardboard hearts. At first I joined in the game with the same enthusiasm as my classmates, but soon got tired of it. I did not like being seen as competing for approval and inventing "good deeds" that I had little inclination for. So I began to bring black stickers to school (most of them invented, I am afraid) and rather enjoyed the consternation I caused.

Looking back on this experience, I realize that my rebellion had very little to do with humility or a sense of my own truth, but more with pride. I decided that being "bad" was more interesting than being good. I thrived on the reputation of being a rebel and on the admiration of my classmates. In other words, it was as much an expression of my budding egotism as striving to win many red stickers would have been.

For true humility lies in a willingness to accept ourselves just as we are: weak or strong, clever or not so clever, timid or brave. It lies in bearing ourselves with patience and trust that God, who created us, does not need us to be anything special in order to love us. Humility lies in our ability to love ourselves as we are and even, if we are really blessed, to enjoy being ourselves.

Invisible Evil

The tendency to confuse egotism with goodness and humility may become a dangerous temptation and an abuse of religion. Some of our spiritual practices or devotions – our good deeds – while admirable in themselves, may not always be expressions of our love for God but ways of feeding our own emotional and ego needs. This may be especially hard for us to face if the practices and devotions we embrace appear to be holy and good. We may feel hurt and offended – and choose not to believe it – if someone tries to convince us that we are abusing religion in order to fulfill our own emotional needs or to gain the approval and admiration of others. And yet this is a temptation that attacks most of us striving to live a spiritual life. We must, therefore, be ready to recognize and resist it.

We may, for example, be too eager to be seen by others as more "religious," more virtuous and more "orthodox" than they are, and let them know it at every opportunity. In other words, we may be using religion to feed our pride and serve the needs of our ego.

We may also develop an excessive interest in miracles, apparitions, extraordinary healings or other unusual events. Such events may occasionally occur, but to rely on them for our faith, to search for them and to be preoccupied with them, is not always a sign of faith and trust in God. It may even be a sign of spiritual laziness or sloth, as it is sometimes called in Christian teaching: an attempt to find a way around the slow, difficult work of inner conversion, the daily effort to find the truth of ourselves and to grow in love.

These various abuses of religion to serve our own egotism can be viewed as manifestations of the sin of hypocrisy that Christ warned us against. Hypocrisy is a dangerous device used by egotism to disguise itself as a virtue and thus to gain the admiration of others and to "lord it over them." Christ called this "the yeast of the Pharisees," perhaps because a little lump of it, one small attempt at self-delusion or pretense, can, if un-recognized and unchecked, pervade and distort our whole spiritual life.

And it is very difficult to recognize and check, especially in ourselves. Not even an experienced spiritual adviser may be able to tell us whether we are genuine in our spiritual life, and we certainly cannot do it alone. As John Milton said in Book III of *Paradise Lost*, "Neither man nor angel can discern Hypocrisy, the only evil that walks Invisible, except to God alone." For this reason it is essential that we be always alert to that danger and pray that God may give us the grace to recognize and avoid it.

Chogyam Trungpa called such misuse of religion to serve one's own egotism "spiritual materialism." He used this expression to describe the condition of those who follow the spiritual path for wrong, "grasping" reasons: those who become preoccupied with acquiring merits, accumulating virtue, searching for extraordinary gifts or experiences and impressing others with their "holiness."[3]

Christians might refer to this same danger as "spiritual greed": a desire to acquire spiritual wealth, to be admired by others – sometimes even by God! – for our virtues and good deeds. We agonize over our failings and sins not always because we are truly sorry for the evil and suffering they may cause, but because they make us look bad.

Archbishop Anthony Bloom used to point out this danger to those who seemed overly concerned about their own spiritual importance. "Why are you making such a fuss about your sins?" he once asked me. "God does not worry too much about your sins. It is your virtues that he finds more difficult to deal with!"

This is a lesson that all of us who try to follow a religious path need to learn: God is never too worried by our sins or too interested in our virtues. The essence of our life with God is not perfection, for that is not within human power to achieve. The essence of our life with God is humility of heart; it is a struggle to be real, to be true to the "self" that God created us be.

34

Motives

It would be absurd to assume that all piety, all striving for perfection, is a result of spiritual greed or hypocrisy. Being mindful of the dangers of egotism should not make us overly cautious or lukewarm in our religious life. For we are called to long and strive for holiness. We are called to "lay treasures for ourselves," but in heaven, not on earth.

It would be equally absurd to assume that to experience any feelings of happiness and joy in our religion would be to succumb to spiritual materialism. If this were so, we would have to cross out most of the names on the list of saints. A complete absence of emotion in religious life would, very likely, not indicate a "higher" spirituality, but might be a symptom of a disturbed psychological condition. It is only when such emotions become the main preoccupation and aim of our religious life that we may be in danger of falling into spiritual greed.

We are often very hard on ourselves. We forget that Christ's command not to judge also applies to judging ourselves (Matthew 7:1). When he condemned those who see a mote in their brother's eye and fail to see a beam in their own, he surely did not mean we should constantly look for every last mote in ourselves and agonize over it. Becoming too scrupulous, rather than diminishing our egotism, may feed it. It may feed our fear of being anything but perfect and right.

We should therefore not worry too much whether our "true" motives for choosing this or that spiritual practice are sufficiently pure, untainted by egotism or spiritual greed. They probably never are totally pure. But worrying about them constantly is not only fruitless, it may be an obstacle on our path. It may be yet another strategy of the ego to keep us all wrapped up in ourselves.

A priest I once knew used to say that nobody ever begins any spiritual practice or takes up any devotion for totally pure, unselfish reasons. But, he would add, that is no reason for not taking it up. Whatever path we follow, if we persevere, if we are attentive to ourselves, and above all to God, we will ultimately begin to see through our ego pretensions and slowly learn how to shed them.

Although discovering our own egotism in any aspect of our spiritual life may be embarrassing for us, although it may seriously hurt our pride and upset our illusions of our own virtuousness, we should see this discovery not as a disaster but as a real grace. Such a discovery – and we shall have to make it over and over again – may lead us to a greater understanding of our own weakness and a greater compassion for ourselves.

For we are all weak. We are all often lonely and in need of belonging. We all want to be approved of, admired and loved. If we accept this truth about ourselves with a little bit of humility and a sense of humour, it will not crush us but free us from a very heavy burden we may have carried since childhood: the illusion that we must be perfect in order to deserve love.

Not to have an ego is the privilege of only very young children or people with certain types of developmental or emotional disabilities, which is why we can learn so much about our true self from them. As adults capable of living an independent life, we cannot get rid of our ego, just as we cannot get rid of any other aspect or expression of our personhood: our body, mind, spirit or soul. None of these are disposable; all have to be nourished and developed, for they all are a gift of God.

Escape from Reality

Thus, Christianity does not view the ego as bad, or false: an aspect of our personhood that we must strive to get rid of. It is only an ego perverted by egotism that is dangerous and unreal. Egotism, because it denies the reality of who we are, affects not only our spiritual life but every aspect of ourselves: our whole life as a person. For whenever and however we deny or forget our true reality, we condemn ourselves to live at the very edge of the void of unreality, of the immense emptiness or absence in our own hearts. As Ursula Le Guin once wrote, "In so far as one denies what is, one is possessed by what is not: the compulsions, the fantasies, the terrors that flock to fill the void...."[4]

When we deny what is and embrace what is not, we live in fear, grasping at anything that might fill this void, always in danger of losing our hold and falling in.

This sense of emptiness and fear is more than our own individual dilemma. It is reflected in the life of our society as a whole, in our social and cultural life: in the way we entertain ourselves, dress, speak, strive to be "different" and to impress or shock each other with our poses and absurdities.

Fascination with magic, clairvoyance, astrology and other ways of searching for some "higher" knowledge or wisdom that we encounter so often today may be manifestations of the same flight from reality. These subjects seem to promise to fulfill the perennial human hope, vain as it has always proved to be, of grasping control of our own destiny and thus becoming "like gods" (Genesis 3:5).

This, in itself, does not make our society unique. Judging by the records and literature of other societies and other times, the temptation to flee from reality has been present in every society and in every age. Yet it seems that in our own contemporary world it is easier to fall into it than it has ever been, perhaps because the means of escaping reality at our disposal are so much more attractive and powerful than ever before.

Our whole lifestyle seems to be based on the illusion that we must become – and have the right to become – something more than we are, although we often do not understand what this "more" really means. Thus we may be easily misled to believe that the creation of a perfect image, perfect appearance, perfect lifestyle – in other words, a perfect ego – is the highest social as well as personal good.

We may be pressured to admire those who, we are told, have achieved such "perfection," however fatuous or neurotic they may be. If we do not resist this pressure we, too, may end up in a wasteland of unreality and egotism that we have created for ourselves, a place where we are alienated from ourselves, from each other and, above all, from God.

When we begin to realize this state of emptiness and alienation within ourselves – as we often do when we experience some great personal failure or pain, and especially when we admit the inevitability of our own death – we may become anxious and depressed, for we do not know how to become free of our egotism and find ourselves again. We do not even know what "being ourselves" means or where and how to begin our search.

The Search for
Self-Knowledge

Many of us living in the contemporary Western world tend to assume that learning the truth of ourselves – true self-knowledge – is, like any other form of knowledge, a rational process: a matter of learning and understanding the facts of psychology, biology or other related sciences and, on that basis, forming the right "scientific" definition of who we are or should be. We assume that we can observe and define our "self" in rational terms.

I certainly assumed that when I was a young student in England. Like many of my fellow students, I started my search for self-knowledge by reading every relevant book on philosophy and psychology I could find. I thought and worried about what my "self" was – probably too often and too much – and endlessly discussed it with my friends, who seemed as obsessed with their own selves as I was with mine. We analyzed all our relationships and tried to understand the causes of everything we did or thought or felt. We assessed our achievements and failures, our "virtues" and faults.

After a few years, it became clear to me that, although I was well informed and well read on the subject of self and had tried to be objective, I still did not know what my true self was. Although I had accumulated many interesting and even helpful thoughts and insights about myself, I still did not know how to relate all I had learned to the unique "I" that I sensed myself to be. I realized that I could not, however hard I tried, examine and analyze my own "I" as if I were looking at it from outside: I could not remove myself from my "I" and study it as an impartial observer.

It is as impossible to study our own "I" as if from outside of ourselves as it is to see our own face directly: we can see it only when reflected in a mirror or captured in a photograph. However helpful and interesting these images may be (and most of us find gazing at our own reflection a fascinating although not always pleasant experience), they do not allow us to see the reality of who we are. It is no longer our own living, self-aware, unique "I" that we observe but an object of thought, an "it." Such an objective self-observation might be a first step to true self-knowledge, but it could never lead me, I realized, to that mysterious inner reality I sensed myself to be.

The Way of Therapy

Some of my friends became convinced that they had found a way of true self-knowledge in psychotherapy and psychoanalysis. They thought that by bringing back into consciousness the forgotten memories and especially the wounds that they had suffered in early life, they could undo the damage and become truly themselves.

Although I never became seriously involved in it, I realized that psychotherapy – and other kinds of psychological counselling – could be very helpful to those who committed themselves to it, that it could make a difference between mental health and emotional instability and distress. It could be an effective way of clearing the ground of anxiety and self-doubt and thus make it possible for us to begin the process of self-knowledge. It could open a way to a better under-standing of our emotional past and a possibility of dealing with it in a more productive and less painful way.

But I also recognized a possible pitfall into which those who take up therapy as a way of self-knowledge could fall, and thus get stuck at that point in their search. There is a powerful, perhaps addictive, attraction in probing and analyzing one's own feelings and wounds. It would be possible – at least for me – to become so fascinated with the process of therapy that the original reason for embarking on it would be lost.

Another potential pitfall is the idea that once we have discovered the roots of our wounds and ills, once we find somebody or something we can blame for them, we will be healed from them once and for all and never again be tormented by them. It would be as absurd to assume that as it would be to assume that knowing what caused a broken leg would be enough to heal it!

This is a dangerous illusion because when it fails, as it most often does, when we discover that we are still the same miserable self we were before, we can be left with a sense of crushing disappointment and discouragement that prevents us from making any further search for the truth of ourselves. To understand the origins of our misery may be an important initial step to finding ourselves again, but we must not get trapped there.

My friends, not surprisingly, thought I was unwilling to enter more deeply into my unconscious because I was too afraid of what I might find there. They may have been right, of course. I might have avoided much confusion and pain later in life if I had listened to their advice. Nevertheless, I became convinced, and I still believe, that even the best and deepest therapy could not lead me to where I really wanted to go: to the heart of my own reality. On the contrary, it might have distracted me from my true inner search.

Which Self?

As I look back on my own efforts to find self-knowledge in those early days, it seems to me that my path would have been much easier if I had understood sooner that what I and my friends were looking for was not our own inner reality, our true self. We were searching for a better, more perfect ego, a more satisfactory persona.

This, I think, is a common misunderstanding of the path of self-knowledge. We approach it not as a way of radical change in the way we understand who we really are, which is the goal of every true spiritual path, but as a way of ego-improvement: of finding an improved, more attractive persona that will be easier for us and others to live with.

I became even more confused when I discovered that I did not have only one such "self." I had acquired quite a few of them! Every time I looked, it seemed, I saw more and more of these "selves" vying for my attention. Not only were they different from each other, they often seemed to be at odds with each other. Which, then, was the real one? Which one should I choose to be?

As I later learned, this dilemma was not unique to me; it is well known to spiritual teachers. What I was experiencing was not a multiplicity of selves but a multiplicity of egos – self-images – that I had acquired, partly as a result of the often contradictory demands and expectations of others but also as a result of my own desire to fit in and fulfill my role in life.

The multiplicity of "selves," unreal as it may be, is still very confusing: not only for us but for others, especially those closest to us. We acquire so many different notions of ourselves and send so many different signals to others, it often becomes impossible to sort them out. This makes all our relationships difficult and may drive us to an agony of confusion and self-doubt.

I experienced such agony many times in my life, especially when I was young and had not yet learned to take myself less seriously. As I look back on who I was then, I cannot help feeling a little sorry for myself and saddened by my insecurity, my desperate search to find a role that would make me feel more significant, more lovable, more sure of myself.

But I never could. Sooner or later each "self" I assumed proved to be just as unsatisfactory, as unfulfilling as another, and I found myself as insecure and confused as I had been before. During one such agony, I went to see my friend Mother Thekla and sought her advice.

"Mother," I asked her, "why do I feel so confused about who I really am? One day I am a religious nut, and the next I am a rationalist, skeptical of all belief. One moment I want to spend my life getting rich and having a good time, and the next I want to be a saint and live in a desert alone! I seem to be always sitting on the fence, unable to decide which side I am on: which of my "selves" is really me!"

Mother Thekla thought for a moment and then said, "Perhaps it is your vocation to remain on the fence! Perhaps you need to find out who you are when you are just sitting in between your different selves."

It was a long time before I began to understand what Mother Thekla meant. She was telling me that I could experience the real truth of myself in those rare moments when I found myself in between my many "selves": when there was a break in the flow of conflicting self-images and inner arguments, a moment of silence amidst the flood of words and ideas that were nearly always jostling in my head. It was at such moments, if I was aware and attentive enough, that I could catch a glimpse of my own true being beyond all my other "selves."

I think that all of us – even the least introspective and most ego-obsessed – experience such moments of the in-between silence. But we rarely pay attention to them: we just let them go. We need to learn how to become more aware of them, enter into them and pay more attention to what is going on within us as they occur. As I was to discover, this kind of awareness and attention could become a powerful means of walking the path of true self-knowledge.

Self-Awareness

The truth of ourselves is hidden more deeply than any thinking or therapy can take us. It is a more profound mystery than words can express. True self-knowledge is not a product of ideas but a way of self-awareness, of being attentive to ourselves: not to who we think we are, or hope we are, but to who we really are. True self-knowledge, we could say, is the way of presence: we find out who we are not by thinking about it but by being present to ourselves, by simply being ourselves.

Because we tend to be so absent from ourselves, so imprisoned in our egotism and inattentive to what goes on in us or in the world around us, it may be hard to understand, or even to imagine, what such self-awareness and attentiveness mean.

This may be especially difficult for Western Christians who, if they think of self-awareness at all, usually think of it in terms of becoming more aware – more conscious – of their own personality or ego, most often in order to fix it or improve it. But self-awareness, as it is understood in most religious traditions, is much more than a way of self-analysis or self-improvement. It is a way of spiritual life.

In recent years, some Christians have become familiar with this more inclusive meaning of self-awareness. There are Christian teachers of self-awareness, and Christian meditation groups that meet regularly to practise this way of prayer and self-knowledge. Yet to many (if not most) Christians, self-awareness still seems rather foreign or un-Christian, perhaps smacking of Eastern religions or even New Age practices.

Thirty or forty years ago, when I first began to explore self-awareness as a way of spiritual life, it could only be learned from one of the major Eastern religions and one had to find a non-Christian guru or master. I followed that path for a time and tried to learn self-awareness from a well-known American Zen Master, Philip Kapleau.

The few years I spent in close connection with Zen Buddhism were very important to me and I am very grateful for them. They helped me to realize the importance of a regular spiritual practice and of the guidance of an experienced spiritual teacher. They taught me to become more aware of what was going on within myself and less bothered or distracted by all the thoughts and ideas that always seemed to play around in my head.

It became easier for me to recognize these distractions for what they were: "just thinking," as Zen masters say; the chatter of a mind that, unable to grasp directly the truth of itself, becomes filled with hundreds of conflicting ideas and assumptions about itself. Zen practice taught me not to become too worried or preoccupied with them but to acknowledge them and then simply let them go: to put them in their proper place.

What Is Now

Zen taught me that the practice of self-awareness is much more than a way of finding some mysterious, esoteric answer to the "problem" of self. It is not a search for an extraordinary mystical experience. Rather, it is an attempt to acquire a new attitude of mind and heart: an attitude of simple, focused attention to everything we do and experience. It is a down-to-earth practice, and it is very hard work.

Some Zen teachers explain self-awareness in this way: "Imagine," they say, "that you are walking down the street totally inattentive to what is going on around you, totally absorbed in your own thoughts and feelings, as we most often are. Suddenly, someone attacks you with a knife. How alert you become in a second! How focused and attentive to everything that is going on within and around you!" The goal of any practice of self-awareness is to learn how to be this alert and attentive every moment of our lives.

In other words, self-awareness is not self-centred: it does not focus exclusively on what is going on inside us. Instead, it opens us up to the whole of reality. It allows us to see that our own inner reality cannot be disconnected from the reality that surrounds us and penetrates every atom of our being. Self-awareness is the ability to be present to what is real, *what is now*.

No one – not even a spiritual master or a saint – can be this aware and attentive, this real, all the time. The main point of this practice is not to search for some permanent state of "higher" awareness or wisdom, but to acquire what the great contemporary Zen Master Suzuki Roshi called "a beginner's mind." We are to learn how to become aware of what is going on within us at this very moment, and be willing to become aware of it again and again.[5]

Self-awareness is a tough and demanding discipline, for it does not allow us to slide into any easy, pre-packaged solutions to our inner search. It demands that we put aside our preconceived notions about ourselves, our illusions of knowing it all, and of being more than we are. Zen is a powerful way of coming to grips with the reality of ourselves.

A Parting of the Ways

Although what I learned as a result of my Zen practice has been invaluable in my life, it became increasingly more difficult for me to continue on a spiritual path that did not have – or did not seem to have – as its goal the search for God. Buddhism is not a theistic religion. It does not profess any belief in God. It might be better to say that it does not address the question of God at all, at least not in the way the biblical tradition understands God: as a Person, a "Thou," as the philosopher Martin Buber put it, with whom we may enter into a mutual relationship of trust and love.

I became convinced that it would be better to leave my Zen group. In retrospect, however, I am not sure I was right. I know now that it is possible to practise Zen wholeheartedly and still remain a deeply committed Christian. I have met several people who have done it and heard about many others.[6] I have also realized that, being the person I am – "always thinking, always checking," as another Zen Master once told me – it might have been wiser for me to persevere in my Zen practice of "not-thinking" for a few more years, if not for the rest of my life.

Yet I can understand why I felt as I did then. I encountered Zen only a short time after I returned to the practice of Christianity and was not yet grounded securely in its tradition of prayer and spiritual life. I had very little knowledge or understanding of the ancient contemplative tradition of the Christian Church. I was not familiar (few Catholics of my generation were) with the central Christian teaching on the Incarnation: of God incarnate at the core of our human reality – the God within– and thus present at the heart of every human being and every spiritual path. The Christian meditation movement and other ways of centering prayer or insight meditation, which might have answered my need for a practice of self-awareness that was also a way of encountering Christ in my own heart, were only just beginning at that time and I knew nothing of them.

It was only a few years later, when I encountered the Orthodox Christian tradition and through it discovered the teaching of the early Eastern Fathers, that I realized that the discipline of inner attention and prayer has been a part of Christian spirituality from the beginning.

But at the time of my parting with Zen I had not yet learned that. It was a difficult step for me to take, as I loved and admired Roshi Kapleau and was afraid he would be disappointed in me. I should have known better. When he learned of my decision to leave his group, Roshi wrote me a letter that I still treasure:"If you feel that your way is Christianity, then you must remain Christian," he told me, "but you must do it wholeheartedly. And, if you do, when the time comes for you to die, all the saints of all the traditions will say, 'The world is a better place, because she has lived.'"

Every time I read these words, I am deeply moved by his wisdom and understanding – but I am also a little frightened, for it seems an awesome responsibility to place on a human being. Yet I realize that it is to such wholeheartedness that all human beings – whatever their beliefs – are called.[7]

I still think of Zen often and miss it in many ways. I miss its clarity and simplicity, the beauty and the silence of the zendo (meditation hall), the companionship and support of the other "warriors" in the battle for true self-knowledge. I miss the courage and energy of Zen masters, which remind me of the courage and energy of the Desert Fathers, those great, tireless "athletes of God."

Most of all, I miss the single-mindedness of Zen, its attitude of "Let us wake up and be attentive! This very moment, now!" All of us – no matter what religion or spiritual path we have embraced – need to wake up from our smugness and spiritual sleep.

Waking Up

Christians need to experience – or recover – this sense of urgency. So many of us seem to spend our lives spiritually half-asleep. We go through the motions that our religion enjoins on us, we try to obey its commandments, we profess our belief in its truth, but there is no real enthusiasm, no real fire in us. We are neither hot nor cold. We need to hear again, as if for the first time, Christ calling us to the same awakening now.

The "waking up" of self-awareness has been compared to becoming suddenly aware of a question we have carried in our hearts for a long time without realizing it, perhaps all our lives. When this awareness strikes, we know we must find an answer to the question; our life will have no meaning unless we do.

"Who am I?" is such a question. We search for the answer in various ways, we ask wise people for insight, we try to figure it out by ourselves. But, sooner or later, we discover that we can never come up with one final answer, and yet we must always, every moment of our lives, keep searching for it.

To be self-aware means to remain in the state of "questioning attention": not yet knowing the answer to the mystery of our existence, but always listening and waiting for it to come to us. It is the only way we can become fully human, fully ourselves.

As contemporary spiritual teacher and writer Michael de Salzman put it,

> Attention...is essentially an act of questioning. This act is the privilege of our human existence. An animal contents itself with being. The responsibility of man is to question himself on the meaning of his being.[8]

Such endless questioning may seem to us both impossible to achieve and of doubtful usefulness. We live in an answer-oriented society that tends to understand all knowledge in terms of clear, precise answers to questions that we ask or are taught to ask. We prefer a ready-made answer to no answer at all. Often we are taught the answer to a question before we even think of asking it. We learn it and thus never need to worry about it again. Once we have the answer – or believe we have the answer – safely stored in our brain or our computer, what would be the point of asking it again and again? Or, if we can never have a certain answer, what would be the point of asking it at all?

It is hard for most of us raised in contemporary Western culture to accept the notion that not all the secrets of existence – our own or those of the universe itself – can be solved by any effort of the mind. It is hard to accept that, at the heart of reality, lies a mystery so deep, so dazzling, so immense, our poor human brains are blinded by its light and can have nothing to say.

Many of us find this not only difficult but even frightening, because it seems to suggest that the world is "irrational": blind and chaotic at its very core. We fear irrationality, for we know how dangerous it can be, how much havoc it has wrought in our world. We fear it especially for ourselves: after all, to become irrational means to become out of control, lost in unreality and ultimately insane.

The Mystery of Things

To say that at the heart of all reality – and so at the heart of ourselves – lies a mystery that cannot be grasped by reason does not mean that existence is irrational or blind. Rather, it points to another dimension of being: another order of reality, as theologians might say. It implies a possibility of knowledge that is not based on evidence but on inner experience of the truly real – of what really is – even when it lies beyond the ability of our physical eyes to see, our hands to touch, our reason to grasp or our language to describe.

This other order of reality does not require some secret knowledge or magical skill to reach. It is ordinary – simple. All children know it exists. They sense it and explore it in the games they play, the stories they read, the movies they watch. But they also see it in their ordinary lives, in the great, mysterious world that surrounds them and that they love to explore. This is the great gift of childhood, the way we may first encounter both ourselves and God. I see it in my grandchildren, I saw it in my own children, and I felt it myself when I was very young.

I remember running into our garden and suddenly stopping in my tracks to stare at the world flooded with beauty, penetrated by a mystery that I had no name for, but that seemed to me wholly and joyfully real. I would enter an empty room on a winter evening and be filled with wonder at the magic that seemed to hide in the shadows thrown by the streetlights outside. I was aware of a mysterious presence behind the old, familiar objects, among the cushions on the couch where my brother and I often played and created our own magic worlds.

This presence did not seem otherworldly or extraordinary to me at all. It was just another dimension of the wonderful mystery of my everyday world. I did not connect it with God. I was brought up in a non-religious family; we hardly ever went to church or prayed at home. The catechism classes that were obligatory at school did not help me make such a connection: we were taught about God in the form of simple answers that we had to learn, often to memorize, and certainly never to question or doubt. If we did, if we asked our instructors, "Yes, but what does it really mean?" we were told not to be a "doubting Thomas" or even sent out of the class in disgrace. It was difficult to relate this God to the moments of mystery I experienced in my ordinary life.

It is only now, as I look back on these moments and remember their fullness, their bright, piercing joy, that I realize these were my first experiences of God: of the world penetrated and filled with the light of God's presence. All my later spiritual adventures, however misguided they may have been at times, never took me far away from the light of that presence.

60

God with Us

As I started to work on this book, a friend asked me if I could write anything without bringing God into it. "Whatever you set out to write about," he said, "you always end up talking about God! Is there nothing more interesting in your life to write about?"

"No," I had to tell him, "there is nothing more interesting in my life than God."

"How can this be?" he persisted. "You have lived through a terrible war, you have seen many places and met many people. Surely you could write about many other things."

"But what would be the use of that?" I asked. "What significance would my life or my 'self' – or any other self – have, what would it mean, unless it was placed within the context of God, who is its origin and end?"

I doubt if my answer satisfied my friend, but I think it was true. The biblical tradition confirms it and makes it absolutely clear: we cannot find our true "I" – the truth at the core of our being – unless we search for it in the presence and light of God. In other words, we can find our true self only in a relationship with God, who alone is the true purpose and meaning of all existence.

The ancient Hebrews do not appear to have worried too much about the "meaning" of themselves. If they thought about this question at all, it was because they understood their total dependence on the ultimate reality of God and sought to understand what God created them to be.

Thus, when the psalmist wondered, "What is man that you should be mindful of him, or the son of man that you should care for him?" (Psalm 8:5), he was not asking a philosophical question about what a human being was. He was reflecting on the question of who God was and expressing his awe at the Divine Glory that shone through all of creation. He was revealing his amazement that God should care for him, a human being, "whose life is like a breath and his days a passing shadow" (Psalm 144:4).

Christianity approaches the question of human existence from the same perspective, but it also adds another, astonishing dimension to this teaching. It insists that God not only revealed himself to us through inspired teachers and prophets, but that, "in the fullness of time," he took on our flesh and became one of us. He is Emmanuel, God with us.

Christ, the Incarnate God, is "the perfect human person," the model of what our life is about. This is the miraculous and amazing nature of the Christian faith. Christ, for whom the whole world was created, "emptied himself" of his divine status, entered our finite, vulnerable humanity and made the human world his own. What's more, he made our innermost reality his own.

Christ in Us

When we stop and reflect on this amazing truth for a moment, we realize its profound significance for our search for the truth of ourselves. The doctrine of the Incarnation not only tells us something about God that we did not know before, it also presents us with an immense – and, for many of our contemporaries, unbelievable – truth about ourselves. The mystery of our self has become the *mystery of Christ*.

To say that the mystery of our self has become the mystery of Christ is to express the fundamental belief of the Christian tradition. For the Good News that Christianity proclaims does not end with the news of God becoming incarnate in the person of Christ and healing the world from its blindness and sin. It does not end even with the promise that, if we remain faithful to him, we shall enjoy eternal bliss with him in heaven.

The Good News is the news of every human being penetrated by the Spirit of God, reproducing in us, although in our finite, human measure, the Incarnation of Christ. Christ is God not only with us but in us: he lives in us, transforming us into himself – not only in eternity but now, today – so that we too may say with St. Paul, "not I but Christ lives in me" (Galatians 2:20). This is the gift promised by Christ as the fruit of love: the gift of God "abiding" in us (John 14:23).

The mystery of the divine indwelling is so immense, so incomprehensible to our reason, that we often shy away from it. We may sometimes glimpse it after communion and occasionally in moments of prayer, but on the whole, we find it easier to think of Christ – and God – as outside of ourselves, in the world, in church, in a statue or a picture on the wall of our room.

Yet, if we want to live the whole truth of ourselves we must, sooner or later, come face to face with that mystery. In Christ, God who is infinite – not bound by space and time – has penetrated our finite human self so deeply, so totally, that the truth of the divine indwelling becomes the most fundamental truth of who we are. In Christ, God is woven into the very texture of our being. We are more closely related to God than a child is related to his or her parents; we are closer to God than identical twins are to each other.

This immense mystery can be approached only in faith. We cannot make ourselves experience it. We can only search for it and pray to be given a glimpse of it. We can try to be alert and attentive to it whenever we become conscious of it. And, once we have experienced it even for a moment, we can never forget it; we can never be satisfied with any path of self-knowledge that does not have as its heart and its final goal a search for God who dwells at the heart of our being and fills us with his life.

Entering the River

Although the mystery of Christ's entering into the heart of our own reality – the mystery of Christ within – cannot be understood or explained in words, it can be approached and experienced in our own lives of reflection and prayer and in the life and prayer of the Church.

One way we can approach this mystery is through icons, the holy images of the Orthodox Church. An icon is not just another form of religious art, which may seem strange and unappealing to our Western eyes. It is not just a representation of a scene in the life of Christ, of the Mother of God or of the saints. Orthodox Christianity considers its icons "sacramental": not only are they powerful means of teaching us the mystery of the events that they represent, but they also contain and confer on us the grace to experience the mystery.

Icons express and make visible to us the mystery of the Incarnation of God; they call us to be attentive to it and to enter its presence. An icon is a place of encounter with the mystery of Christ. When we pray and reflect on an icon we not only think of the event it presents, or try to imagine it in detail (although some people find that helpful), we try to open ourselves – our whole being – to it and to the presence of Christ that an icon mediates.

An icon, however, does not only call us to be attentive and to open ourselves to the truth of Christ. It also calls us to be attentive to the truth of ourselves. For this is the miraculous and amazing nature of the Christian faith that all true icons reflect: that because in Christ God has taken on our whole humanity except sin, he bears in his own humanity – his own self – the truth of each person's self. Christ is present at the heart of each: beyond all the egos, all the disguises, all selfishness and sin. The truth of Christ is our own deepest truth.

This truth has been brought very clearly to me in Mother Maria Gysi's reflections on the icon of the Baptism of Christ in the Jordan.[9] Christ stands in the depths of the riverbed, the gap between two high rocks. On one side is our human shore – our human reality – where John the Baptist, whom Christ called the greatest of men, stands to baptize Christ and be the first witness to his truth.

On the other side lies "the shore of heaven where the angels tenderly await his return." Christ descends out of his divine infinite reality into the gap that divides us from eternity, so that he can share his own divine life with us.

This icon has become very familiar to me. I have it in front of me as I write. I see the shores and the river that flows between them: the dark river of earthly reality and, or so it seems to me, the river of forgetfulness and sin that is now made holy by the presence of Christ. He stands on the water rather than in it. He touches upon it lightly; it does not engulf him, for he is the Lord. The Spirit of God descends upon him and the light of heaven surrounds him.

And now, Mother Thekla's advice – that to find my true self I must find and encounter the reality in between all my egos and personas – makes sense to me as never before. I see that the reality she referred to was not only the place of an encounter with my own true self, it was also the place to which I must eventually come in order to know who I truly am. It is the gap of the Jordan: the gap between my own finite reality and the infinite, incomprehensible reality of God. It is this gap that Christ came to bridge when he descended into my deepest self.

Because the Man Christ is also God who dwells with us and, even more radically, is within us; when we find Christ, we also find the heart of who we are. When we encounter Christ, when we are given even a glimpse of his presence "abiding in us," our heart "leaps for joy" and begins to burn within us. It is only then that we may begin to understand what our self truly is and why the saints have said that when we find our true heart, we find both ourselves and God.

Finding Our True Heart

The heart we must find is not the physical heart or the heart as the symbol of our emotional life. It is the heart as the biblical tradition understands it: the core of our whole being, of our whole life as a person.

The heart is where we are truly ourselves – where our true "I" resides. From there all of our selves – good and bad – all our moral decisions, all our actions, thoughts and words flow. As Christ said, it is in the heart that the real truth of each person can be found (Matthew 15:10-20). This is why it is possible to say that to find our heart is to find the reality of who we are.

The *Catechism of the Catholic Church* expresses and summarizes this mystery in these words:

> The heart is our hidden center, beyond the grasp of our reason and of others; only the Spirit of God can fathom the human heart and know it fully. The heart is the place of decision, deeper than our psychic drives. It is the place of truth, where we choose life or death. It is the place of encounter, because as image of God we live in relation: it is the place of the covenant. (no. 2563)

It is this sense that the Bible refers to when it speaks of a "trusting heart," a "listening heart," a "loving heart" or a "lying heart." For the heart is not always true or good; it may be wicked and deceitful; it may be cold, like a stone. The decisions we make are not always life-giving. We can, the whole biblical tradition makes clear, choose death.

And yet, the biblical tradition says, the fundamental truth of ourselves – our "true heart" or "heart of hearts" – is never really taken away from us. It is the name that God breathed into us at our creation. It is our true self that we can, and most often do, forget and obscure with our egotism, spiritual blindness, anger or hate. But even when obscured or denied, it is always there and we can always find it again.[10]

St. Augustine wrote in his commentary on the Gospel of John that we are exiles from ourselves, for we do not know ourselves. In order to know ourselves we must return to the heart.[11] Finding the heart is not a way of study and thought, nor a way of some esoteric knowledge about ourselves, nor any extraordinary way of being more spiritual or holy. It is the path of constant, patient returning to the truth of ourselves.

This may not be an answer we had hoped to find; it may never fully satisfy our thinking and defining mind. It does not tell us in rational terms or explain in plain language what our "I" really is. It may tell us that who we are now is not the best self we can ever be and that we must change. But it also tells us that we can change, that we can find our true heart again. There, in the depth of our own being, in the silence of attention, we may begin to experience the true reality of ourselves.

Being a Person

To return to the heart does not mean to become a fragment of ourselves, however central and true this fragment may be. The heart – the "I" – is as inconceivable by itself as the hub of a wheel would be without the spokes or the rim it supports. Without the spokes or the rim, the hub would not be a hub but a surrealist absurdity. The true self is our whole self, all of ourselves, freed from egotism and sin and converted – turned back – to God.

This may not be obvious to us at first, because we have been exposed too often to the belief that human beings are composed of separate parts or aspects – body, mind, soul and spirit – some of which are not as important or "holy" as others.

In that scheme of things, the body is usually assigned the most inferior status. At best, it is only a shell in which our true identity – our spirit or soul – is enclosed and which is discarded at death. At worst, it is a distraction and a source of temptation and sin.

It is therefore important to keep in mind that, as many prominent Christian teachers, including Pope John Paul II, have reminded us in recent times, Christianity does not support such a view of human nature. In fact, it considers this interpretation a heresy that crept into Christian religious thought at an early stage and has reappeared in one guise or another ever since.

It is a heresy because it contradicts the teaching of the biblical tradition – both Hebrew and Christian – that in order to remain a person, we must retain or regain the whole of our humanity: every aspect of ourselves, the body as well as the soul and the spirit. In a way we cannot understand or imagine, we must remain – even after death – fully embodied and thus fully ourselves.[12]

The body is not merely the outer casing of our spiritual side, but an essential aspect of being human that grounds and connects us to the whole physical universe. We cannot get rid of it for good and remain a complete human person, a self. It is on this conviction that the belief in the resurrection of the body is based.

This belief has been and remains a scandal to many. We may be scandalized, too. We may find it challenging or even impossible to believe. It would indeed be impossible to believe if not for our faith in the divinity of Christ. It is only when we believe that Christ was both fully divine and fully human – a fully human person – that we can also believe that, at some unimaginable moment at the end of time, in a way we cannot now comprehend, we shall participate in his victory over death in the totality of our own unique and inalienable human personhood.

Eternity of Love

Christian insistence that our personhood survives our bodily death – the belief in the immortality of the human person – delivers us from a terrifying possibility: dissolution of our "I" at death. And yet, not all of us find it easy to accept such a deliverance. Some of us may even find it unbearable.

It often seemed unbearable to me when I was young; the burden of being always separate and, therefore, always alone felt very heavy to me then. The thought that I might have to carry it for all eternity seemed an outrageous and frightening possibility.

One of the reasons I was drawn to Zen was that it seemed to offer an escape from such an "outrageous" possibility. It appeared to offer a hope that one day, in some future life – and, if I worked and practised very hard, even in this one – such an escape could be found. In the end, death could become truly *final*: it would be the door through which I could enter into the great non-personal – higher than personal – "ocean of being" from which I came and to which I would now return.

I still struggle with the persistent desire to lay down the burden of my individual personhood – my body, my soul, my stormy emotions and restless brain

– if not in this life, at least in eternity. I do not always feel glad at the thought of remaining forever the person I am, however special and unique I may be.

Yet, as I get older and my earthly self is giving me more and more signals that it may soon give up on me for good, I am surprised to realize that I do not look forward to being freed from it so much anymore. I am grateful to God for having known better than to make me more than a person, or bodiless.

Without my own separate, embodied personhood, I could not have experienced the joy of living in the world, a joy that has been greater than all its suffering and fear. I could not have known the miracle and beauty of nature; the wonder of great music, literature or art; the excitement of learning and thinking; the pleasure of talking with friends or eating great food. There would be no children or grandchildren in my life!

Without personhood, all those who have died, even the Mother of God herself and the most glorious of saints, would have disappeared into this "ocean of being." Without personhood, there would be no communion of saints, no one to pray to for guidance and support as we journey to God. Above all, there would have been no Christ waiting for us at the end. There would not have been any resurrection: Christ risen from the dead, somehow different – transformed – and yet still the same. Without personhood there could not have been any love, for only a person can really give oneself to another in love. And, without love, what kind of eternal life could there be?

At the core of the Christian understanding of eternal life lies the conviction that love is the nature of eternal life. Eternal life – heaven – is love. This love is personal: self-aware, fully present and open to God, to each other and to all of creation. Eternal life is a way of total presence and total love. In other words, it is a way of total communion with God and the whole of creation.

But, someone might ask, what about those who do not believe in Christ? How can they enter the life of communion with God and find the whole truth of themselves? We cannot answer that question, for none of us can presume to know or has the right to decide or define the path of fullness of life and self-knowledge for another. Yet there is one truth that surely applies to us all: it is impossible to find the true meaning of one's life without love.

If we do not love, we remain selfish, imprisoned in our egotism and spiritually blind, no matter what beliefs we profess. Only when we open ourselves to the heart of another can we open ourselves to the truth of our own heart and find our true self. As Christians, we can also say that because God is love, whoever loves another also knows God and shares in the same mystery of love: God's love for us and our love for God. Love – our "ordinary" human love – is a royal way to self-knowledge.

76

Conversation with God

The mystery of our being is the mystery hidden in God. Only God, who alone can fathom the human heart, knows who we really are and who we are still to become: a person fully alive, fully penetrated by the life of Christ (see 1 John 3:2). We can learn the truth of ourselves only from God. And this means only in prayer.

For too many of us, prayer seems to be a one-sided affair. It is a way of talking to God (or at God) in the hope that our words and petitions (or complaints) will somehow find their way and be heard through the immense distance that lies between us and God. We may also think of prayer as contemplation, a way of thinking and reflecting on God.

Such an understanding of prayer is only partly true. We must, of course, ask God for all we need; Christ himself told us so. We must praise and thank God for everything God has done for us. It is good to think about God and reflect on our relationship with God.

But this is not the whole truth that Christianity teaches us about prayer. According to the Scriptures, theologians and, even more significant, the real experts on prayer – the saints – true prayer is not a matter of thinking or talking: it is a matter of listening. It is an opening of our innermost being to God.

Prayer is not a monologue, it is a conversation. As Evagrius of Pontus wrote in the fourth century, "Prayer is a constant intercourse of the heart with God. There is no greater thing than to converse intimately with God and to be preoccupied with his company."[13] Many centuries later, St. Teresa of Avila echoed this same truth when she said, "Prayer is a conversation with the Beloved."

To have a conversation, we must be with another person; we must be truly present and attentive to each other. True presence involves much more than being in the same place; after all, we can be, and often are, physically present to somebody and yet miles away from them in our heart.

To be really present means to be fully turned towards each other, fully engaged. It does not always mean talking to each other, for sometimes more is said in silence, but being with each other in love. True conversation, therefore, is an encounter of love, because to be truly present and open to another person is to love that person.

Thus, to say that prayer is a conversation with God is to say that prayer is an encounter between two persons – two selves: our own small, finite, hardly aware self and the infinitely loving, infinitely knowing, infinitely aware Self of God. In the words of St. Thérèse of Lisieux, "Prayer is a surge of the heart...a cry of recognition and of love" (*Catechism of the Catholic Church* no. 2559, note 1).

Perhaps we have experienced moments of such recognition in a human relationship, in moments of friendship and love. We recall the sense of ease and familiarity that such love brought us, and the assurance that we were truly known and accepted just as we were. This allowed us to be ourselves in a simple, direct way that we had not done since we were children, if ever. For we are most open, most truly at home, most childlike, when we are loved.

If that is true of human relationships, it is infinitely more true of our relationship with God. When we pray – when we are in conversation with God – our hearts are at peace, and we can see and accept ourselves, if only for a moment, as children do. Not because we have come to believe that we are perfect or "good" (for, as we know, children are not always perfect or good), but because we have begun to realize that it is possible and all right for us to be only ourselves.

Heart of a Child

To see ourselves as a child sees – to have the heart of a child – does not mean forgetting all we have learned and experienced since childhood, all the good or evil that has been done to us or that we have done. How absurd that would be! Nor does it mean becoming simplistic and naive, or acquiring yet another ego, adding childlikeness to our repertoire of roles. Rather, it means being willing to put aside all our roles, drop all our masks and see ourselves in the way my grandson Joseph saw me – with all my "bags and wrinkles": my weaknesses, pretenses and fears. We become like children and enter the kingdom of heaven when we learn to accept ourselves and trust ourselves, when we learn to live out of our own real self again.

Yet we cannot help but realize how far away we are from that goal, how great are the obstacles we encounter. We do not know how to accept ourselves and become real. We carry a heavy burden of disappointment, resentment and, perhaps the heaviest of all, mistrust. We may have become like children who, because they cannot trust their parents' love for them, are also unable to trust themselves or anybody else, not even God. We have moments of peace and insight, moments "in between" when we glimpse the real truth of ourselves, but we cannot hold onto them for long. We are easily tempted back into our egotism and all the unhappiness and fear that it brings.

Perhaps my daughter Kathryn expressed this problem most clearly for me when she was six or seven years old. As we drove back to our cottage after an afternoon spent at Madonna House, Kathryn turned to me and said, "Mrs. Doherty says that she always prays for the heart of a child. And she gets it, too, for God always does what she asks him to do! But, as soon as she gets it, her heart starts growing up again!" She sat deep in thought for a while and then turned to me and said, "Mommy, that means she can never stop praying for it!"

The heart of a child is the gift we can never stop praying for; in this life, we can never hold onto it for good. We can never learn to trust either God or ourselves for good. Our egotism, our spiritual blind-ness, has become rooted in our souls and has put out – and is still putting out – many new shoots. We cannot uproot them all in a day or even over many years. This task will keep us busy for the rest of our lives. This is why, as Catherine Doherty also said, we must pray every day not only to have the heart of a child but also to be given the "awesome courage to live it out." For the burden we carry is not only of our own doing but of the whole of humanity.

The Human Condition

In the Christian tradition, egotism and all the un-happiness and evil that may follow from it are understood as the tragic consequence of the Fall: our first parents' refusal to be satisfied with the self that God had created them to be and their unwillingness to accept their reality as creatures. They who, by the fact of their personhood, were made to be "above the rest of creation" still could not bear to remain "a little lower than the angels" (Psalm 8:6) and to submit to the conditions of their embodied earthly life. As a consequence, they lost their own true identity and became not more than themselves, but less.

Having turned away from God – unenlightened by the light of God's presence – they became blind to the true nature of themselves. They fell into what Western Christians usually call original sin and the Orthodox Church prefers to call the "human con-dition": the state of humanity separated from God. They became alienated from God, from each other and from the whole of creation. They were filled with guilt and mistrust, blamed each other and felt compelled to hide their shame.

Whether we think of this narrative as a historical event or as a spirit-filled – inspired – sacred story presenting a fundamental truth of our human reality, its essential significance for us is clear. The story of the Fall teaches us that deep at the roots of human existence lies a tragic and mistaken choice that has affected and continues to affect us all. For, according to traditional Christian teaching, all human beings have inherited the same tendency to turn away from reality and embrace the unreality of egotism and pride.

Such a belief may be difficult, even impossible, for many Christians to accept. It may seem preposterous to believe that God, who is love, would make us responsible for a sin committed in a distant past and make us suffer its consequences forever. This interpretation seems not only to offend our sense of justice and even our common sense, but also to negate our inner conviction that in order to be truly human we are free to choose our own destiny.

And yet, living as we do in the age of great scientific discoveries about the human organism, especially in the area of human genetics, we are more aware than ever before that we are not always masters of our own destiny. We carry burdens that we cannot avoid, limitations we cannot overcome, an inherited destiny we have done nothing to deserve and cannot really control. Not only our upbringing and history, but our genetic makeup – our bodies, minds, temperaments and inborn abilities – bear the consequences of who our ancestors were and what they have or have not done.

Whether we like it or not, we are inheritors of the reality – good and bad – of others, and we, in turn, are creators of the reality of all who come after us. We cannot avoid or deny this fact; we must face it and deal with it with as much courage and faith as we can.

We may find this truth difficult to face: not only does it seem to strip us of our human dignity and make us feel powerless, it also seems to contradict the concept of freedom, on which the whole of Christian moral teaching is based. If we have inherited the consequences of our first parents' choice, and of the choices of countless others since then, how can we say we are free to choose our destiny and are responsible for our lives?

Free to Choose

Freedom of choice – free will – cannot be demonstrated by science or by any rational argument. Even religion cannot claim to prove it "beyond a reasonable doubt." We must choose to believe in it.

To believe in our freedom – that is, to choose to see ourselves not as helpless victims of circumstances but as free and responsible human beings – is the most fundamental choice we must make in life. It is an existential choice, for we make it on the basis not of any external evidence or proof but on the basis of our own inner experience of ourselves: of our own "I."

This choice lies at the very source of our search for the truth of ourselves. For if, on some level of our being, we did not already know ourselves to be fundamentally free, what would be the point of our search? If we believed that who we are was predetermined long before we were born, we would have to conclude that nothing we could learn or do about it could lead to change. We would have no choice but to be as we were made.

Yet our own inner experience or religious convictions and the experience of countless others teach us that we do have such a choice. People in prisons, people in concentration camps, people forced to live in terrible conditions, undergoing great suffering and loss, have been able to hold onto their conviction of freedom even in the face of death.

They discovered, as we must discover, that although they could not control their living conditions, their emotions and even, perhaps, their state of mind, although they may have been forced to do or say what they knew was wrong, they could still choose to face the reality of their circumstances in their own true way. They could hold onto their inner truth, refusing to believe the lie that they were worthless, rejected or abandoned by God. They could refuse to despair. They could refuse – and keep refusing – to hate.

Few of us will be asked to undergo such a test. But all of us are asked over and over again to refuse to submit to our own negative emotions: our fear, our resentment, our need for reassurance and praise. We are asked to struggle with them, to turn away from them and to choose love. For true love cannot be forced – not even by our own compulsive desires and needs. It can only be offered freely, as a gift. Love is a free gift of our being. When we love, we are free. This is true of human love, but especially of a loving relationship with God.

When we love God and have experienced God's love for us, we cannot have any doubt that we are free: free to love and be loved by God, free to choose to be ourselves, free to be free! And yet, free to choose must also mean free to refuse to believe in God's love. We can, like our first parents, choose to trust the devil – the voice of our egotism – rather than God. This is the fundamental choice, the fundamental temptation that we have to reject, not just once, but again and again.

Dismantling of Egotism

There are many paths for returning to the truth of ourselves; human beings have followed these over the centuries. But there is one path that countless Christians have walked and experienced: the path of recognizing and "dismantling" – letting go of – all that is not real in ourselves. We discover what is true by discarding what is not true, what is false.

Or, we might say that we return to the truth of ourselves as it were "negatively," by stripping off all the masks and disguises we have been hiding behind.[14] In other words, the path of self-knowledge is a slow, patient work of dismantling our egotism: of divesting ourselves of all the protective layers we have wrapped around ourselves and thus slowly regaining the simplicity of heart we had as children.

In Christian teaching, approaching the truth of ourselves (or any other spiritual truth) by recognizing and rejecting what is not true is known as the apophatic way – the way of negation. We discover what is true by discarding what is not true, what is false. Thus, we cannot answer the question "Who is God?" The infinity of God cannot be grasped by the human mind. But we can say what God is not: God is not finite, or indifferent, or changeable, for example. To assume otherwise would be a contradiction in terms.

In the same way, we can never fully answer the question "Who am I?" directly, for the mystery of our self lies beyond where reason can observe it or define it in words. We can, however, often recognize what we are not. We are able to know when we are being untrue to ourselves. There seems to be a sense of our own truth hidden deep within us; otherwise, how would we know that we are being untrue?

This sense of truth – of reality – is the voice of our conscience. It is the inner law of our nature that God has implanted in our heart (Romans 2:15) so that we may grow into our full stature as the persons we were created to be.

The truth of ourselves lies too deep for us to reach with our thinking mind or learn from another person. Yet it is always there, like a sound ringing at the heart of our being alerting us to the fact that we are "off," not true to ourselves – that something we do or say or think is false. And when we realize that, we do not argue with it; we do not agonize over it; we acknowledge it and let it go.

This is not a path of some heroic spiritual effort or inspired wisdom, but the patient, daily struggle to find and remove what is not real in ourselves so that we can uncover and encounter what is real. It is a struggle to "empty ourselves" (Philippians 2:7) of all that is false and distorted in us and to become true to our whole, unique human personhood. Above all, it is a way of prayer – of listening to God – who alone is infinitely real, in whose presence all unreality withers and dies. In other words, it is the path of ceaseless conversion: of re-turning to the reality of being only ourselves again and again.

The Path of Conversion

The concept of ceaseless conversion is at the heart of Christian life, but it is largely unknown or misunderstood by modern Western Christians. If we think of it at all, we think in terms of converting from one faith to another, a rare, once-in-a-lifetime event. In traditional Christian teaching, however, conversion refers to the whole Christian life: a life of turning away from our habitual false way of being and returning to our true identity, our true self.[15] Conversion is the path of constant, patient returning to the centre – the true heart – of ourselves. It is a path of returning to Christ who lives at the core of our being and transforms us into himself. It is a path of longing, prayer and love.

Conversion is a painful path to walk. It has been called "white martyrdom," for none of us likes to face our own unreality and egotism, our weaknesses and faults, and to acknowledge them, even to ourselves. We become very tired of having to dismantle the disguises and masks that we have assumed and keep assuming over so many years, of having to let go of our strategies and endless games.

I began to learn that truth very early in my spiritual life when, during a summer visit to Madonna House in Combermere, Ontario, I returned to the practice of Christianity I had left behind – I was sure for good – more than twenty years before. My conversion was not a result of some intellectual conviction or argument, but a deeply personal experience of an encounter with Christ so powerfully present in the life of that simple and apparently very ordinary community.

It was only much later that I began to appreciate the price that each member of the community had to be willing to pay in order to make God so present to all who sought him there. To be "a light to your neighbour's feet," as foundress Catherine Doherty often described the Madonna House vocation, you must be willing to face and struggle with the darkness in yourself.

But I did not think of such things that first summer, for I was having the most wonderful time of my life. I was convinced that at last I knew who I truly was; that I had been healed from all my blindness and egotism and that from then on I would have no trouble loving myself and every other person in the world. I went around grinning at everybody and everything, overflowing with pious emotion and generally very pleased with myself.

I often talked about all the wonderful things that were happening to me with Fr. Emile Brière, the person who was most instrumental in my conversion and who would become my spiritual father and beloved friend for over thirty years. Fr. Brière – or Fr. B, as most of his friends called him – was a man of great spiritual wisdom and experience, but also of great tenderness and simple, down-to-earth common sense. He had a sense of humour that I did not always appreciate at first but soon came to enjoy and share. I learned to trust him and to rely on his discernment and advice.

A Kind of Death

I especially remember one conversation I had with Fr. B that summer. I was relating to him all the spiritual experiences and insights I was having, thinking that he would be thrilled and pleased, perhaps even impressed, with the spiritual progress I was sure I was making. I was therefore surprised and a little hurt when, instead of praising me, Fr. B burst out laughing and said, "I am glad you are having such a good time. Enjoy it while you can, for it will soon pass!"

Seeing how disappointed I looked, he hugged me and explained, "All those feelings and thoughts are nice to have, but they are only feelings and thoughts and do not last. It is not wise to hang on to them or imagine that they are the real stuff. The real stuff, most often, does not feel so good at all! Conversion, you will find out, is not a joy ride but a kind of death."

It did not take me very long to discover how right Fr. Brière was. The life of conversion truly is a kind of death. As we dismantle one layer of self-deception and egotism after another, we are never sure what we shall find underneath it all. The illusion that the ego is our only self may be so deeply rooted in our minds that, whatever our faith or our inner experience tell us, we may never completely let go of the fear of dissolution into nothingness.

Conversion may seem even more frightening to us if we have come to believe that the Gospel calls us to work towards the "death" – the dismantling – not only of our egotism but of our whole self; when we imagine that in order to become truly Christian we must give up our natural human life, that we must reject our desire for happiness and fulfillment of our human needs. Many of the Christian teachers and writers on asceticism, especially in the past, seem to have understood it as such.

It would be unwise and presumptuous to reject or belittle such an interpretation of the Christian vocation to holiness that has been embraced and lived by countless saints. It would be absurd to forget the goodness and the overflowing charity that many of these men and women showed in their lives.

Nevertheless, it is important to remind ourselves that such a way of heroic virtue is not the only way open to us. When we feel discouraged by the endless struggle with our own weakness and fear, we need to remind ourselves, like Fr. B reminded me countless times, that the life to which Christ has called us is not a way of hate and rejection but a way of love. It is better to do a little out of love than to do much out of fear of rejection or a sense of guilt.

Three days before his death in June 2003, Fr. Brière, who was already drifting in and out of consciousness and hardly able to breathe, suddenly opened his eyes and said, "All I have ever wanted was to learn how to love." I cannot imagine or hope for a better death.

The Will of God

Christ himself never spoke of the death of self. When he called us to deny ourselves, to take up our cross and follow him (Matthew 16:24) he did not ask us to deny or give up our love of life or our search for happiness but to return to our true reality. He called us to depose ourselves – not only our ego, but our whole self – from the central place in our lives. In other words, and this, I think, is the heart of the Christian tradition of holiness, Christ called us to deny the priority of our own self and our own will over the will of God: to love God more than ourselves.

Christ's call to self-denial is the call to choose God's way over our own even if it means death, as it did for him. In some mysterious way, we are to reverse the choice our first parents made and to keep reversing it every moment of our lives through ceaseless conversion. He called us to accept and trust our human reality and live it fully, without counting the cost. We do not need to seek a more painful kind of dying than that.

Few of us have not been profoundly moved by the scene of Christ's agony in the Garden. To think of him, the Son of God, alone and afraid, sweating blood and begging God to take the chalice away from him, goes far beyond what we can understand or imagine. To hear him cry out in his agony, "Father, let your will be done, not mine!" is to stand before a mystery of a relationship that we can never understand and yet are drawn to reflect on.

I cannot think of that scene without realizing that each one of us must enter that mystery in our own life to the degree that we receive the grace to do so. What Christ accepted with these words was not only the reality of his own suffering and death, but also the reality of our whole human life.

He accepted it all – the glory and the terror of it – in our name, as we must now accept it in his. Not to accept it – to choose our own version of what reality "should be" – would be to fall into the hell of unreality and self-delusion that Christ came to reject and conquer. He knew that we can be ourselves only when we accept the whole of our reality: the whole of God's mysterious will for us and for the world.

Faced with this immense mystery, we begin to understand: the will of God that we need to seek and embrace is not some mysterious and arbitrary set of laws or decrees that might demand of us a violation or denial of our own reality. The will of God *is* our reality. To conform ourselves to the will of God means conforming to the deepest truth of ourselves, the truth that our own minds can never imagine and our wills can never fully grasp. It means opening ourselves to the infinite reality of God's eternal presence and love in our life as well as in our death.

Guilt and Repentance

But how do we begin the work of conversion? How do we learn to return to the reality of who we are? We need to begin, I think, at the point at which we are the weakest, the most tormented, the most unreal. For many of us, that point lies in our addiction to the strategies of guilt and blame, which we seem to have acquired long before we grew up. Only very young children do not know these strategies, because they have not yet learned to fear being only themselves. It is when we learn this fear that we take the first step away from the innocence of childhood.

This innocence always surprised and disarmed me in my own children. I remember one occasion when I was unhappy with my son for something he had done. "This was a naughty thing to do!" I said to him. Mathew, who was playing with his toys on the floor, looked up at me, sighed deeply and agreed. "Yes, Mommy, I know," he said, and went back to his toys. He did not offer any excuses, he did not blame anybody. He even seemed to take my scolding to heart, but he did not appear unduly dejected by it or crushed with guilt.

None of us, children or adults, needs to be crushed with guilt, for the sense of guilt that torments us and gnaws at our hearts is nearly always based on illusion, not on truth. An exaggerated and debilitating sense of guilt – a sense of self-contempt or even self-hate – could of course be a symptom of psychological illness and may need to be treated as such. But it may also be a dangerous spiritual condition, a symptom of egotism and spiritual pride, an expression of our inability to accept being human: vulnerable and weak, easily manipulated to forget and even deny our own truth.

Such guilt, however, should not be confused with what the early Christian teachers called "compunction": an acute and often painful sense of responsibility for the sins we have committed and the harm we have done. Compunction does not lead to the torment of guilt and self-hate but to repentance.

Repentance is an essential aspect of the life of conversion. We cannot even begin to live it unless we first acknowledge and ask forgiveness for the wrongs we have committed and try to make amends for them. When we repent, we acknowledge the reality of ourselves, take responsibility for what we have done or failed to do, and resolve to strive not to do it again. But we do not hate ourselves and torment ourselves with guilt; we surrender ourselves to the mercy of God.

For true repentance is always a way of prayer. Repentance does not make sense outside of a relationship with God. Only when we are in God's presence and are given even a glimpse of the infinite nature of God's love and mercy can we truly repent.

We see our weakness and sin, our self-centredness and all the other symptoms of our egotism and we repent for them: we surrender them all to God. We are free of them. In repentance we "spit at the devil," as the Orthodox Church expresses it. Repentance is a way of self-knowledge, not of self-obsession and blame.

The torment of guilt, on the other hand, does not help us get to know ourselves better or make it easier to let go of the disguises and pretensions of our false egos. Rather, it makes us hide ourselves even deeper in our delusions and wrap ourselves in them even more tightly. Guilt makes us want to justify ourselves at all costs, reassure ourselves that what we have done or what we have become is not our fault. It is our parents' fault, or our society's, or the Church's, or the fault of whomever else we may resent and feel badly done by. We become addicted to self-justification and blame.

Dealing with Guilt

Guilt, in the sense we use it here, is very difficult and painful to recognize and address because it is always based on fear: fear of inadequacy, of being marked forever for rejection and blame. Whenever we are overcome with guilt, all our relationships become wrought with the possibility of disappointment and hurt. Guilt may paralyze us and make us unable to think clearly or make difficult decisions, especially ones that can have no perfect or painless solution.

Some years ago, I was struggling with a decision that seemed unavoidable but was proving impossible to make. I could not face the upheaval and suffering I knew it would cause. I could not bear the thought that I might be blamed for every consequence it might bring about. So I did nothing. Meanwhile, things became more painful and difficult every day.

Finally, my friend Leo, who knew me well, came to see me and tried to talk some sense into me. "What do you think you need to do in this situation?" he asked. "I know very well what I must do," I answered, "but the thought of doing it fills me with dread. When I think of all the suffering it might cause and how awful it would make me feel, I am paralyzed with guilt."

"Well, I know what to do," Leo said. "Do what you would do if you felt no guilt at all, and I shall feel as guilty as you want while you are doing it!" "How can that help?" I asked him. "And who do you think you are: Christ returned to earth?" "Well, why not?" he replied. "Is it not what he has told us to do: bear each other's pain? Try it. What have you got to lose?"

So I tried it. I did what I knew I had to do as if I did not feel guilty at all, and imagined I gave my guilt to my friend to hold. I suffered nearly as much as I thought I would and Leo said it was hell, but it did not kill either him or me.

We both knew, of course, that this was only a "trick," a game we were playing to help me get unstuck from the paralysis of guilt and indecision. We knew that no friend, however close and willing he or she might be, could take away anybody's guilt. It was God to whom I needed to surrender it; God could not only hold it for me for a while but also free me from it for good. But we do need to be Christ to each other sometimes. As my friend pointed out, this is what Christ has asked us to do.

I have used this technique – I might call it my "holy game" of pretending that I do not feel guilty, or rejected, or just "no good" – very often since then and have shared it with others. It works, I have found, not only with guilt but with every negative emotion or thought. Whenever one of them begins to torment me and threatens to overwhelm me, I have learned not to argue or struggle with it on my own, but to acknowledge it and surrender it to God, who can deal with it much better than I ever could: I "de-sting" it, as Mother Maria Gysi used to say. I turn it into prayer and deprive it of its victory.[16]

A New Beginning

Our life of conversion – our struggle to accept and embrace God's will – never lets us fall into the illusion that we are "all done," perfect, or that we might ever be. It is a painful way and yet, when we have walked it for a while, we begin to realize what a marvellous gift it is. We experience a new kind of stability and peace that we could not find any other way.

We also begin to experience a sense of freedom and lightness of heart – not only as an idea or a principle of belief, but with our whole being. We realize that, however far and estranged from the truth of ourselves we might be, our daily, painful struggle has freed us from the most agonizing fear of all: the fear of being rejected and unloved. We are overwhelmed by the immensity of love and mercy God has shown us by calling us to this life. We have discovered the way of true love.

No relationship of love, no true "conversation" – with another human being and, above all, with God – is possible unless we are willing to surrender daily the illusions, disguises and false assumptions that arise in any relationship. In order to find love we must be willing to face and let go of everything in ourselves that is not love: we must be willing to be converted every day of our lives.

Eventually it becomes clear to us that this vocation, this work of conversion, is the only way we can undo the consequences of our first parents' sin; it is a new beginning on the path that human beings were created to walk but from which they had fallen away.

I have never been able to believe that we were created by God only to live forever in an earthly Paradise, happy and contented but always the same. I know that I at least could not really be satisfied with such contentment and happiness; I would soon be bored. Above all, I asked myself, in such an unchanging, endless earthly life would I – would anyone – ever be able to reach out towards heaven, to long and search for it?

The biblical account of creation does not involve itself in any "what if" situations; it does not explain what would have happened if our first parents had chosen to obey God. But the fact that we were created free to choose (and therefore also free to refuse) sug-gests that an untroubled, endless existence might not have been the final end of creation. It allows us at least to suppose that we were created to become what Adam and Eve would have become if they had only trusted God enough, if they had refused to listen to the Father of Lies and let God do things his own way. To become fully ourselves – whether in earthly para-dise or in earthly hell – we must choose to be so.

The Fall was such a tragic and needless mistake! Without it, our first parents – and all human beings after them – could have become everything they could have desired or imagined. They could have grown into an ever-fuller union with God, become ever more like God and thus more fully themselves. It was their choice to make and they turned away from God.

Yet Christian tradition assures us that in spite of this mistake, which has affected each one of us deeply and made our own choices much more difficult, we have not irretrievably lost the chance to become what God intended. In the Person of Christ, we have been given yet another chance to start over again.

Christ came to open to us again the path to the fullness of life, but he did not do so all at once. Accepting Christ is the essential beginning, but not the end, of the Christian path of conversion. We have not been made any more perfect or any less capable of making wrong choices than our first parents originally were, and we shall surely make wrong choices again and again. We have only been given another chance to begin the path to perfection, another chance to grow into the fullness of life that is our inheritance as God's children.

The Whole Truth

My sense of guilt, and all the other addictions of egotism I have acquired over the years, never quite left me, but they have become less troublesome every year. I now become aware of them sooner than I did in the past, and find it easier to dismantle them. I have learned to let go of my need to justify myself and to blame others for my failings and fears: to take responsibility for who I am.

Taking responsibility for who we are does not mean overlooking or denying significant and formative ways others have treated us in the past, especially in childhood. Indeed, we must realize and accept that we may not have been loved enough, appreciated or understood. We may have been rejected or even abused; we may truly have a lot to forgive.

Yet if we are ever to learn how to forgive and be healed, if we are ever to find ourselves again, we must also understand the role we have played in allowing ourselves to become "false": in forgetting or denying our true self. We must accept our share of responsibility for who we have become. Those who have hurt us must find their own way of facing themselves and healing, too, but that is between them and God. Eventually, we may even learn to want to pray for them as Christ told us to do, but that is the work of grace. Our part is to realize that blaming them does not bring us closer to the truth of ourselves: nor does blaming ourselves or tormenting ourselves with guilt.

Taking responsibility does not mean blaming anybody at all. It means accepting the reality of who we are. In order to find the truth of ourselves we need to learn how and why we may have contributed to our self-forgetting: why we so often denied – and continue to deny – our own truth. When we are willing to ask such questions and to face the whole truth of ourselves, we have begun to walk the way of self-knowledge. We have begun the work of finding our true heart again.

For it is not only outside pressures that lead most of us to forget or deny our unique gift of personhood and retreat into our self-protective strategies. It is also the fear that lies deep in our own hearts – all the more dangerous because it is most often unconscious – of what it means to be a person created by a unique, never to be repeated act of God. This is the fear of being always fundamentally alone: separated from others by a chasm that cannot be bridged by an act of will or any effort of the mind or any human act.

The Fear of Aloneness

I t may be difficult for us to believe in the existence
of such fear in ourselves if we think of aloneness
mainly in terms of either solitude or loneliness. Thus
we may insist that we like being alone, that we need
periods of solitude and rest from the tasks and demands of our daily lives. And this is clearly so. We all
need, and some of us need it more than others, to
take a holiday from our everyday roles and disguises
and get reacquainted with ourselves. Above all, we
need to take time to get reacquainted with God.

Loneliness, on the other hand, is an experience
that none of us seek. It can be described as an intense
feeling of sadness, of being homesick for someone
we love or a place we have left behind. Most of us
have experienced this feeling and have found it
painful and difficult to bear.

Yet aloneness may be experienced in an even
more painful and frightening way: as a sense of rejection, of being unloved, of literally being left alone.
This is much more painful than loneliness, because
being lonely can often be remedied by seeking the
company of others or getting involved in some
common activity, whereas aloneness is a state of being over which we have no control.

Such a persistent and disturbing sense of aloneness is often viewed as a psychological condition: a consequence of early childhood experiences that have coloured our emotional lives ever since. Abandoned and unloved children often experience this aloneness. So do people with disabilities. So do prisoners and refugees. And so do many elderly people.

Aloneness is a common and often unavoidable condition of old age. Our children have grown up and have lives of their own. Our spouses, our relatives and many of our friends are dying or have already died. We live in our suddenly empty houses, our apartments, cottages or nursing homes, very aware of how alone we have become and how little we can do to change this situation. We may find this a frightening and, at times, overwhelming experience.

Most acutely, we all experience this state of mind when faced with the reality of death: the death of those close to us and especially our own death. For we cannot help but realize that however beloved and befriended we may have been in life, nobody can do our dying with us: we must die alone. This, for many of us, may be the most terrifying aspect of death.

The fear of aloneness, however, is not only a psychological or emotional reaction to unfortunate circumstances or conditions, but a natural and vitally important fear that all human beings share, whether we are aware of it or not: we cannot survive in this world alone. This is why during most of human history, banishment was feared even more than death.

Aloneness is especially dangerous and terrifying to children. A child who has been abandoned, rejected and left alone is in fact sentenced to death – if not physically, then psychologically. Even if this abandonment was unintended or temporary, the fear a child experiences at this moment may remain in the child's memory – and the memory of his or her parents – forever.

Even the thought of ever having to abandon our child or having our child snatched away from us is a nightmare that haunts every parent. The fact that many children have been abandoned in our world is so terrible to think about that most often we prefer to ignore it. It triggers in us not only horror and compassion but also our own forgotten insecurity and fear.

Never at Home

As I look back on my life, I realize that it was such a sense of aloneness – of being separate, different from others – that has been at the centre of my long struggle to know myself. For me, the question "Who am I?" could only be answered in the context of this aloneness. If I could not learn to understand and come to terms with it, I could not come to terms with myself.

It is not surprising that aloneness has been a significant factor in my life. Growing up in Europe during the Second World War, I became aware at an early age of the capability human beings have for evil and hatred. Like most children in similar situations, I developed a sense of caution and self-protectiveness and found it difficult to trust and open myself to others.

Then, at the end of the war, as a young teenager, I became a "displaced person" and an exile from my native Poland. I had to leave behind my home, my friends, and all the familiar sights, sounds and smells that were part of my everyday life. Eventually I found myself in Britain, among strangers whose language I could not speak, whose way of life was foreign to me, and who could not understand or even imagine the world I came from.

Although I learned English very quickly and seemed to settle down happily in my new life, I never lost that feeling of being an alien, separated and different from the people among whom I lived, never quite at home. I did not question this sense of aloneness while I was young – I assumed that it was part of being a war survivor and a foreigner and that I had to make the best of it. It did not cripple me or prevent me from enjoying and treasuring life, following my various interests and making friends.

It was only many years later that I began to understand that my sense of aloneness reached much deeper into my being than I had thought. It was more than the result of my having been transplanted in my youth; it was more than a peculiar and, at times, painful personality trait: it was a fundamental reality of all human existence. It was an expression of an existential aloneness: the condition of being a human person, a unique and self-aware "I." It was the unavoidable aspect of the life that we must live on earth.

In the deepest sense of the word, we are alone from the moment we are born, although we might not become aware of it for a long time. This knowledge may creep into our awareness in moments of weakness or sorrow, rejection or defeat. But we may also experience it in moments of happiness and joy, in the presence of the people we love when we suddenly realize that we really do not know them at all, that they are, in a fundamental way, separate from us.

113

We cannot escape or deny our aloneness, for it is real: it is a part of the human condition that we entered when we were born. We cannot pretend that it is not painful or even frightening. We cannot always help trying to run away from it, to fill it with every distraction and noise, to cling to anyone or anything that may help us forget that it is there.

But we can refuse to run away from it for good or to view it as a fruit of our own failure, an inescapable doom laid on us by God – our own living hell. We can choose to enter and embrace it as a place of communion and love. For that is indeed what it is. Aloneness – our inherent uniqueness and separateness from others – is an inner desert at the very heart of ourselves reserved only for God. It is a place of true solitude: a place where we encounter God and discover to our never-ending surprise and delight that when we are at home with God, we are also at home with each other and with the world.

The Desert Within

The desert has been an important place of prayer and self-knowledge in all religious traditions for many centuries. Even now, we may hear of ordinary and quite sane adults leaving their homes and going to live in the desert somewhere to seek solitude, silence and an encounter with God. Others may seek their desert experience in hermitages, monasteries or retreat centres. They are looking, they may say, for a place where they can learn how to be at peace with themselves and with God.

To find a desert, however, we do not need to go to a special place. As Catherine Doherty wrote in her book *Poustinia* (the Russian word for desert), "Deserts, silence, solitude are not necessarily places but states of mind and heart."[17] In our inner poustinia – our inner aloneness – we can find all the silence and solitude we want. We must find it within ourselves, enter it and stay there for as long as we need and as long as we can bear.

For the desert, whether it is a physical location or our own inner reality, is a painful and dangerous place. When we enter the desert, we do not leave the rest of ourselves outside. We bring with us all that we are. To be in the desert means opening ourselves to the whole of our reality: its pain as well as its joy.

Guilt, temptations, crazy thoughts and painful memories that we thought we had already dismantled assail us again and again.

I once heard a story of a young monk who went to the desert to spend the rest of his life there alone, in fasting and prayer, exploring his heart and searching for God. He had been there only a few weeks when he was seen running out of his hermitage screaming with fear. He could not bear it any longer, he said, for the devil tormented him all the time and would not let him pray. He was brought to an old, experienced hermit who looked at him with compassion and said, "Ah, my friend, it was not the devil, it was only yourself!"[18]

I do not remember what happened to the monk in the end. Did he return to the desert? I hope he did, for, as most of those who have experienced their inner desert will tell you, in order to get rid of the many devils that torment us there, we must find the courage to face them.

The inner desert is always with us. We enter it to face our aloneness and to open ourselves fully to it. Entering it does not mean giving up our ordinary life, for the desert is, or soon becomes, an integral part of our daily existence. We enter it every time we become aware of our aloneness and pain – a situation that will happen more and more often as we learn to be more attentive to ourselves.

We did not choose our aloneness when we were born, but we can choose it now. Instead of hiding from it, we can decide to become aware of it and pay

116

attention to it. Aloneness is the truth of ourselves, the core of our personhood. It is the place – the gap of the Jordan – between our human finiteness and the infinite being of God that is our vocation, our work in life, to enter and to explore.

Ceaseless Prayer

For many of us, going into the desert may also be the only way we can truly learn how to pray – and to "pray ceaselessly," as St. Paul urged the Thessalonians to do (1 Thessalonians 5:17). Ceaseless prayer does not consist of saying endless prayers – the more and the longer the better – but of being present to God wherever we are and whatever we do. Ceaseless prayer is a relationship of love.

That, in a very real way, means being alone with God. In order to enter a relationship of love – to be truly present to another – we have to do it alone. For love is the relationship of one separate, unique person to another. Love is not total absorption in another, it is not emotional dependency; it is being always present, always aware of and available to another.

We learn to pray ceaselessly by being alone with God, by turning to God again and again in a movement of love and trust, until our prayer becomes a ceaseless, even unconscious movement of our heart. This is the kind of ceaseless prayer that the desert can teach us. Sometimes we learn it – we are led to it – by weakness and fear, as the following story tells us.

There was once a great and holy man who had lived in the desert for many years and was greatly admired for his ceaseless prayer. One day his disciples asked him how he had learned to pray so well. It was easy, he told them; the desert itself had taught him.

When he was a young man, he said, he had heard a priest describe the wonderful life of ceaseless prayer that St. Paul preached and the saints living in the desert taught their disciples to practise. So, there and then, he decided to give away all his possessions and go to the desert to live in silence and find out how to pray and never stop praying. And that is what he did.

He walked through the desert for a while till he found a spot where he thought he could pray undisturbed. There were some bushes behind which he could find shelter at night and a pool of clean water close by. And so he settled down to pray the night away. No sooner had he begun when he heard a terrifying roaring and howling coming from behind the bush where he lay. The young man shook with fright and his teeth chattered. "Lord Jesus, have mercy on me!" he begged over and over again. The roaring, however, did not stop till morning. He spent his first night in the desert shaking and calling for help.

When the morning arrived at last, he was very tired and longed for a drink. "It is daylight now," he said to himself, "so it is safe to go and have a drink from the pool." But then another thought stopped him in his tracks: the animals that had terrified him all night might also be thirsty and go to the pool to drink! But, in the end, he became so thirsty that he was forced to go. He was very frightened, and he shouted, "Lord Jesus, have mercy!" all the way.

This went on for many nights and days. Then, one day, he realized he was not afraid anymore. The animals had become his friends and did not keep him awake. But he kept on praying because, he said, by then he could not stop! He had learned the secret of unceasing prayer.[19]

We, too, often begin to pray in earnest only when we face a difficult and painful situation: when we feel afraid, helpless and alone. But this should not surprise or distress us unduly. The most important thing is that we have begun to pray; one day we may discover that we are no longer able or willing to stop. The desert is still a desert, and we are still alone, but our aloneness has become not a place of loneliness and fear but a place of communion with God, with ourselves, and with the whole of creation. We are truly at home.

Poverty of the Heart

As we live a life of ceaseless prayer and conversion, as we dismantle layer after layer of self-delusions and disguises, we come face to face with what we have feared most (and now realize never needed to fear): the poverty of being only ourselves.

We look at ourselves in the presence of God and we begin to understand why Christ called such poverty "blessed." Having stripped ourselves of all that is not ourselves, having nothing left to cling to or hide behind, we begin to experience more clearly every day why only the poor can enter the kingdom of God. To be poor in spirit means to be willing to cling to nothing, to possess nothing but God.

For most Christians, and for many followers of other spiritual traditions, St. Francis of Assisi is the best-known example of such poverty. According to one story I heard many years ago, God asked St. Francis of Assisi to dance in the city square of Assisi before his horrified family and gaping fellow citizens. St. Francis was terrified and begged God to ask him to do something else – anything but that. He was only a beggar; he was dirty and covered in rags. How could he face such embarrassment and shame!

But God was relentless and Francis danced. At first he could hardly move; his body seemed to be made of lead and his heart about to explode. But as he forced himself to go on, his body relaxed, he danced faster and faster and a song of joy burst from his lips.

Like the good citizens of Assisi, I too was horrified when I first heard this story. I prayed desperately that nothing like that should ever be asked of me. I would have preferred, I think, to do anything, to lose everything I had, rather than to become such a fool and expose myself in such a way!

But I have learned that, sooner or later, God asks us all to become foolish. God asks us to strip ourselves of some disguise or self-image we have built and have clung to for most of our lives, and thus to uncover our most hidden fear or shame. Even the healthiest of us, the most emotionally stable and mature, may have something within us that we fear to face and fear even more to reveal.

The stripping of such a disguise is a personal thing, and each of us must come to it in our own way. It is a matter between us and God. Yet, if we want to be truly ourselves, sooner or later God will take us at our word and show us what we are hiding from and what we must do. And, sooner or later, or so we hope and pray, we shall do what God asks.

At first, like St. Francis, we stagger around blindly, we stumble and fall; we appear to others – and to ourselves – to be totally absurd. But before long we, too, begin to relax and to hear an inner music – the music of our own souls – and we are filled with joy. We understand at last that what God really wants for us is to lose all our fear and discover the freedom of being poor in heart.

Only Between Me and God

Although we cannot hope to reach the poverty of heart or the holiness of St. Francis, most of us have probably experienced moments of such inner poverty and ultimately the freedom and joy they brought. We need to remember these moments and reflect on them often, for they let us touch the deepest truth of ourselves.

I experienced one such moment a few years ago when I found myself in the emergency department of the local hospital. I was lying on a high hospital bed surrounded by all kinds of equipment, connected to all kinds of machines. Doctors, nurses and lab technicians came in and out of the room, probing me with needles and checking the machines. The friend who had brought me there stood at the foot of my bed looking terrified.

I do not remember feeling frightened myself, although I do recall thinking that this might be the end. But I felt detached from it all, as if it were happening to someone else. Suddenly, a thought as clear as a bell came into my mind: "There is nobody here except me and God. I do not have to explain myself or justify myself to anybody ever again. My life is, and has always been, only between me and God!"

And sick as I was, a sense of exultation and over-flowing relief burst out at the centre of my being. I looked at the white hospital walls, at the needles stuck into my body, at the machines humming by my bed, at the face of a nurse bending over me and I laughed aloud. "I am alone with God," I thought, "and I am free!"

At that moment I understood what a terrible burden I had carried for most of my life. I had looked to my parents, my teachers, my friends, even my enemies, to define me, to judge me and tell me who I am. Now I knew that the only true judgment to be passed on me would take place between me and God.

I knew that when I had left everything behind, when at last I was truly alone with God, he would show me the truth of myself – all I was, all I had been, all I had done – and ask me whether I was ready to accept it. Could I embrace myself as I really was: poor, fallible, weak and yet beloved of God? Or would I turn away and fall back into the unreality of self-condemnation and self-hate that is hell? I knew this was the only judgment I would ever have to face.

My health crisis turned out to be a false alarm, of course. I was soon sent home with a few prescriptions and warnings of doom. While my "dying" experience was a powerful one, what I learned from it has often been difficult to remember and to live. I still often need to explain and justify myself to myself and to others. But every time I remember that amazing experience I know that what I learned then is true: I am indeed "only myself," and there is nothing else I would rather be.

Endless Becoming

Once we begin to accept our unique, separate personhood as our own true life, we also start to see what an immense gift it has been to us. Our life has not been always easy, always good or free from suffering and sin, but it has been our life – our own irreplaceable human journey on earth. Every step we have taken on it, every moment we have experienced, has not been a random event, but a step to who we are now, in this moment. It has been a step on our true path of self-knowledge, a step on our way to God.

We know that we are still the same "I" we were at the beginning, the same person we were when we were born. And yet we are also more than we have ever been or could imagine being; we are incomparably richer and more fully alive. We are still the same and yet we are always new. We have learned to enjoy being only ourselves.

But, I sometimes think, we learn to enjoy this fully only in old age. As we grow older, we find that we are a little less hard on ourselves, less worried about our failures and imperfections, less willing to judge ourselves. We are ready to embrace our aloneness, our times in the desert, our fear of final rejection and failure to "deserve" love. It becomes easier to accept our own inner poverty, which we had feared so much. We realize that we have never been really alone; that never, not even for a split second, has God been absent from us; that nothing we have done or that has been done to us has been able to separate us from the love of God.

We are therefore also ready to accept the mystery that we are, and must remain, even to ourselves. Our search for the truth of ourselves can never end, because we can never exhaust all the possibilities that were opened to us at the beginning. For it is the fundamental nature of being human, being a creature, that we are never perfect, never complete: not in this life and perhaps not even in eternity. We can never say, "Now we are all we can ever be." We can never reach the final goal of total presence, total love, total communion with God.

We begin to understand that our attempts to assume a more perfect ego contained, like all human errors and illusions, a small particle of truth. For we *are* called to become more than ourselves: we are to become holy, full of splendour and grace. We are called to enter the River Jordan: the in-between of our human reality, between earth and heaven, and to "put on Christ," as the Eastern Church sings again and again on the Feast of the Baptism of the Lord and at every baptism. We are called to become ever more like Christ living within us, ever more filled with God.

God, towards whom we are moving, for whom we are searching, is inexhaustible. Heaven and earth cannot contain God. We can never know, love or enjoy God enough. This is what eternal life may turn out to be: not only an end of every pain, sorrow and fear, but also an endless becoming, an endless growing in knowledge, love and joy. We have been created for the joy of always becoming more and more fully ourselves, the joy of never-ending conversation with God.

Notes

[1] In Christian thought, the term "human nature" refers not only to our physical or instinctive needs and desires but to the whole of our being – body, mind and soul – that is, our whole human self. We are never asked to deny or suppress it or strive to transcend it in order to reach some supernatural state. We are only asked to open ourselves to the supernatural – that is, the divine – action of God.

[2] Mother Thekla is an Orthodox nun who lives in England. She is the first spiritual daughter of Mother Maria Gysi, an Orthodox writer and a spiritual mother to many. Mother Thekla has been a good and wise friend to me during the last twenty years.

[3] See Chogyam Trungpa, *Spiritual Materialism* (Boston: Shambhala, 2004).

[4] Ursula K. Le Guin, *The Lathe of Heaven* (New York: Avon Books, 1973), p. 146.

[5] Shunryu Suzuki, *Zen Mind, Beginner's Mind* (New York: Weatherhill, 1970). He was one of the first Zen masters to come to North America. *Roshi* is the Japanese title given only to a recognized Zen teacher or master. The English word "mind," as used in Zen Buddhism (as in the phrase "Zen mind"), refers to the mind as the centre not only of thought, but also of spiritual knowledge, wisdom and love. It is therefore possible to compare it to the Christian notion of the "heart." See the chapter in this book entitled "Finding Our True Heart," and note 10 below.

[6] In fact, my interest in Zen came first from reading Thomas Merton and, later, Fr. William Johnston S.J. More recently, I discovered the work of Sr. Elaine MacInnes, a Canadian nun

who became a recognized Zen master in Japan and later taught Zen to many Westerners. Her autobiography, *Zen Contemplation: A Bridge of Living Water* (Ottawa: Novalis, 2001), is, I think, a must read for Christians interested in Zen meditation.

[7] As I was writing this, I received the news of Roshi Kapleau's death at the age of 91 in May 2004. He died peacefully on a sunny afternoon in the garden of Rochester Zen Center, surrounded by his students and friends.

[8] Michael de Salzman, "Awaken to the Question" in *Parabola,* vol. 27, no. 1, p. 56. De Salzman died in 2002.

[9] Mother Maria, *Realism of the Orthodox Faith* (Toronto: Peregrina Publishing Co., 1975) pp. 9–10.

[10] Teaching on the heart as the core of a human person can be found in the whole Christian tradition. Western Christians, however, do not assign the same central importance to it as the Orthodox do. Thus, for example, apart from the passage quoted above, the *Catechism of the Catholic Church* refers to the heart as the "depths of one's being" only in one sentence at the end of its chapter on the soul (no. 368). Yet the notion of the heart is not absent from Western Catholic piety and life. It is often mentioned in prayer and liturgy. The popular devotion to the Sacred Heart of Jesus and, more recently, to the Immaculate Heart of Mary, whatever we may think of some of its external manifestations, points to the same fundamental insight into the human reality. It is not the physical heart of Christ we seek and revere, but the very core of his humanity.

[11] Augustine, *Tractate on the Gospel of St. John*, 10, 1–2. I owe this reference to my brother, Fr. J.A. Ihnatowicz, of the University of St. Thomas, Houston, Texas, whose advice has been very helpful to me in writing the more theological sections of this book, although I did not always follow it. Thus he cannot be blamed for any errors I may have committed.

[12] Originally, early Christian writers understood the soul (*psyche* in Greek) as Aristotle had understood it: as that which makes any being alive and specifically itself. In that sense

131

every living being – humans as well as animals and plants – have a "soul." Human beings, however, have a rational soul: a soul that is open to the spirit and capable of knowing and loving God. It is also, according to Christian teaching, a soul endowed with immortality.

The spirit is usually viewed by Western Christian theologians as the soul's spiritual dimension, which makes us capable of communion with God (*Catechism of the Catholic Church*, no. 367). Orthodox thinking, however, tends to consider it as a separate aspect of the human person that links us most directly with the spiritual reality. (Kallistos Ware, *The Orthodox Way* [Crestwood, NY: St. Vladimir's Seminary Press, 2002], p. 28.)

[13] Evagrius of Pontus, *On Prayer*, n. 35. I owe this reference, as well as the reference to St. Teresa's definition of prayer, to my brother.

[14] The original meaning of dismantling was "taking off a robe or cloak."

[15] *Metanoia*: the Greek word translated as conversion or repentance means literally a "change of mind" (or "heart"). See also Irma Zaleski, *Conversion of the Heart* (Ottawa: Novalis, 2003).

[16] For a fascinating, and I think very helpful, discussion of negative emotions and a way of dealing with them written by a psychotherapist who is also a Buddhist, see Tara Bennett-Goleman, *Emotional Alchemy: How the Mind Can Heal the Heart* (New York: Harmony Books, 2001).

[17] Catherine Doherty, *Poustinia* (Notre Dame, IN: Ave Maria Press, 1975), p. 21.

[18] This story and the two in the next two chapters are told from memory. I have been unable to trace their origin.

[19] In the Eastern Christian tradition, ceaseless prayer is known and most often practised as the "Jesus Prayer" – the silent repetition of the words "Jesus Christ, Son of God, have mercy on me, a sinner." See Irma Zaleski, *Living the Jesus Prayer* (Ottawa: Novalis, 1997).

Other books by Irma Zaleski

Who Is God?

In *Who is God?* Irma Zaleski suggests how we can open ourselves to God and then how we can learn to live in God's presence. She also points out the path that we are called to follow in order to become the true images, or icons, of God that we have been created to be. Yes, difficulties and doubts may torment us on the way, but the journey to God, our soul's home, is ultimately a joyful one.

Mother Macrina

A set of refreshing yet meditative reflections. Using the fictitious character of Mother Macrina, Zaleski creates "teaching tales" featuring a wise, modern Desert Mother, resonant with the Eastern monastic tradition. The thoughtful prose is complemented by evocative woodcut illustrations.

Conversion of the Heart
The Way of Repentance

Drawing once again on the Eastern Christian tradition, Zaleski invites us to deeper knowledge of God's infinite forgiveness and mercy, taking a way largely neglected and obscured in the West. This is the way of repentance: a constant attitude of heart, going beyond regret to healing, from guilt to liberation.

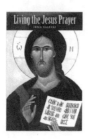

Living the Jesus Prayer

An ancient devotion in the Eastern Church, the Jesus Prayer is now becoming more familiar to Christians in the West. This slender volume is the perfect introduction to this time-honoured meditative prayer.

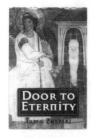

Door to Eternity

This hopeful, insightful book looks at the mystery and certainty of death and the faith and hope that we can bring to it – not only our final bodily death at the end, but also our daily death of self that, as Christians, we are all called to undergo. As Irma Zaleski believes, "The mystery of death points to a possibility of joy and glory so immense, so exciting, and so infinitely beyond anything we can ever dream of or imagine, that it is worth giving up our life for it."

To order these and other fine books, contact

NOVALIS

1-800-387-7164 or cservice@novalis-inc.com